elevate science

SAVVAS
LEARNING COMPANY

You are an author!

This is your book to keep. Write and draw in it! Record your data and discoveries in it! You are an author of this book!

Print your name, school, town, and state below.

My Photo

Name _____

School _____

Town, State _____

ISBN-13:   978-0-328-94875-8
ISBN-10:   0-328-94875-6
9 21

Program Authors

ZIPPORAH MILLER, EdD

Coordinator for K-12 Science Programs, Anne Arundel County Public Schools

Zipporah Miller currently serves as the Senior Manager for Organizational Learning with the Anne Arundel County Public School System. Prior to that she served as the K-12 Coordinator for science in Anne Arundel County. She conducts national training to science stakeholders on the Next Generation Science Standards. Dr. Miller also served as the Associate Executive Director for Professional Development Programs and conferences at the National Science Teachers Association (NSTA) and served as a reviewer during the development of Next Generation Science Standards. Dr. Miller holds a doctoral degree from University of Maryland College Park, a master's degree in school administration and supervision from Bowie State University, and a bachelor's degree from Chadron State College.

MICHAEL J. PADILLA, PhD

Professor Emeritus, Eugene P. Moore School of Education, Clemson University, Clemson, South Carolina

Michael J. Padilla taught science in middle and secondary schools, has more than 30 years of experience educating middle grades science teachers, and served as one of the writers of the 1996 U.S. National Science Education Standards. In recent years Mike has focused on teaching science to English Language Learners. His extensive leadership experience, serving as Principal Investigator on numerous National Science Foundation and U.S. Department of Education grants, resulted in more than $35 million in funding to improve science education. He served as president of the National Science Teachers Association, the world's largest science teaching organization, in 2005–6.

MICHAEL E. WYSESSION, PhD

Professor of Earth and Planetary Sciences, Washington University, St. Louis, Missouri

An author on more than 100 science and science education publications, Dr. Wysession was awarded the prestigious National Science Foundation Presidential Faculty Fellowship and Packard Foundation Fellowship for his research in geophysics, primarily focused on using seismic tomography to determine the forces driving plate tectonics. Dr. Wysession is also a leader in geoscience literacy and education, including being chair of the Earth Science Literacy Principles, author of several popular geology Great Courses video lecture series, and a lead writer of the Next Generation Science Standards*.

Reviewers

Program Consultants

Carol Baker
Science Curriculum

Dr. Carol K. Baker is superintendent for Lyons Elementary K-8 School District in Lyons, Illinois. Prior to that, she was Director of Curriculum for Science and Music in Oak Lawn, Illinois. Before that she taught Physics and Earth Science for 18 years. In the recent past, Dr. Baker also wrote assessment questions for ACT (EXPLORE and PLAN), was elected president of the Illinois Science Teachers Association from 2011-2013 and served as a member of the Museum of Science and Industry advisory boards in Chicago. Dr. Baker received her BS in Physics and a science teaching certification. She is a writer of the Next Generation Science Standards. She completed her Master of Educational Administration (K-12) and earned her doctorate in Educational Leadership.

Jim Cummins
ELL

Dr. Cummins's research focuses on literacy development in multilingual schools and the role technology plays in learning across the curriculum. *Elevate Science* incorporates research-based principles for integrating language with the teaching of academic content based on Dr. Cummins's work.

Elfrieda Hiebert
Literacy

Dr. Hiebert is the President and CEO of TextProject, a nonprofit aimed at providing open-access resources for instruction of beginning and struggling readers, and a former primary school teacher. She is also a research associate at the University of California Santa Cruz. Her research addresses how fluency, vocabulary, and knowledge can be fostered through appropriate texts, and her contributions have been recognized through awards, such as the Oscar Causey Award for Outstanding Contributions to Reading Research (Literacy Research Association, 2015), Research to Practice Award (American Educational Research Association, 2013), William S. Gray Citation of Merit Award for Outstanding Contributions to Reading Research (International Reading Association, 2008).

Content Reviewers

Alex Blom, Ph.D.
Associate Professor
Department Of Physical Sciences
Alverno College
Milwaukee, Wisconsin

Joy Branlund, Ph.D.
Department of Physical Science
Southwestern Illinois College
Granite City, Illinois

Judy Calhoun
Associate Professor
Physical Sciences
Alverno College
Milwaukee, Wisconsin

Stefan Debbert
Associate Professor of Chemistry
Lawrence University
Appleton, Wisconsin

Diane Doser
Professor
Department of Geological Sciences
University of Texas at El Paso
El Paso, Texas

Rick Duhrkopf, Ph. D.
Department of Biology
Baylor University
Waco, Texas

Jennifer Liang
University Of Minnesota Duluth
Duluth, Minnesota

Heather Mernitz, Ph.D.
Associate Professor of Physical Sciences
Alverno College
Milwaukee, Wisconsin

Joseph McCullough, Ph.D.
Cabrillo College
Aptos, California

Katie M. Nemeth, Ph.D.
Assistant Professor
College of Science and Engineering
University of Minnesota Duluth
Duluth, Minnesota

Maik Pertermann
Department of Geology
Western Wyoming Community College
Rock Springs, Wyoming

Scott Rochette
Department of the Earth Sciences
The College at Brockport
State University of New York
Brockport, New York

David Schuster
Washington University in St Louis
St. Louis, Missouri

Shannon Stevenson
Department of Biology
University of Minnesota Duluth
Duluth, Minnesota

Paul Stoddard, Ph.D.
Department of Geology and Environmental Geosciences
Northern Illinois University
DeKalb, Illinois

Nancy Taylor
American Public University
Charles Town, West Virginia

Safety Reviewers

Douglas Mandt, M.S.
Science Education Consultant
Edgewood, Washington

Juliana Textley, Ph.D.
Author, NSTA books on school science safety
Adjunct Professor
Lesley University
Cambridge, Massachusetts

Teacher Reviewers

Jennifer Bennett, M.A.
Memorial Middle School
Tampa, Florida

Sonia Blackstone
Lake County Schools
Howey In the Hills, Florida

Teresa Bode
Roosevelt Elementary
Tampa, Florida

Tyler C. Britt, Ed.S.
Curriculum & Instructional
 Practice Coordinator
Raytown Quality Schools
Raytown, Missouri

A. Colleen Campos
Grandview High School
Aurora, Colorado

Ronald Davis
Riverview Elementary
Riverview, Florida

Coleen Doulk
Challenger School
Spring Hill, Florida

Mary D. Dube
Burnett Middle School
Seffner, Florida

Sandra Galpin
Adams Middle School
Tampa, Florida

Margaret Henry
Lebanon Junior High School
Lebanon, Ohio

Christina Hill
Beth Shields Middle School
Ruskin, Florida

Judy Johnis
Gorden Burnett Middle School
Seffner, Florida

Karen Y. Johnson
Beth Shields Middle School
Ruskin, Florida

Jane Kemp
Lockhart Elementary School
Tampa, Florida

Denise Kuhling
Adams Middle School
Tampa, Florida

Esther Leonard M.Ed. and L.M.T.
Gifted and Talented Implementation Specialist
San Antonio Independent School District
San Antonio, Texas

Kelly Maharaj
Science Department Chairperson
Challenger K8 School of Science and
 Mathematics
Elgin, Florida

Kevin J. Maser, Ed.D.
H. Frank Carey Jr/Sr High School
Franklin Square, New York

Angie L. Matamoros, Ph.D.
ALM Science Consultant
Weston, Florida

Corey Mayle
Brogden Middle School
Durham, North Carolina

Keith McCarthy
George Washington Middle School
Wayne, New Jersey

Yolanda O. Peña
John F. Kennedy Junior High School
West Valley City, Utah

Kathleen M. Poe
Jacksonville Beach Elementary School
Jacksonville Beach, Florida

Wendy Rauld
Monroe Middle School
Tampa, Florida

Bryna Selig
Gaithersburg Middle School
Gaithersburg, Maryland

Pat (Patricia) Shane, Ph.D.
STEM & ELA Education Consultant
Chapel Hill, North Carolina

Diana Shelton
Burnett Middle School
Seffner, Florida

Nakia Sturrup
Jennings Middle School
Seffner, Florida

Melissa Triebwasser
Walden Lake Elementary
Plant City, Florida

Michele Bubley Wiehagen
Science Coach
Miles Elementary School
Tampa, Florida

Pauline Wilcox
Instructional Science Coach
Fox Chapel Middle School
Spring Hill, Florida

Motion and Forces

Quest

In this Quest activity, you meet a game designer who wants your help to design a new game.

Like a game designer, you complete activities and labs to evaluate how different forces cause a ball to move in different ways. You will use what you learn in the lessons to design a new game in which you collect points while you keep the ball from rolling off a surface.

Find your Quest activities on pages 2–3, 13, 23, 32, 40–41, 42

Career Connection Game Designer page 43

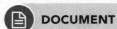
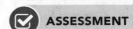

VIDEO

eTEXT

INTERACTIVITY

VIRTUAL LAB

GAME

DOCUMENT

ASSESSMENT

The Essential Question

HANDS-ON LAB

3-PS2-3, 3-PS2-4, 3–5-ETS1-1

Electricity and Magnetism

Quest

In this Quest activity, you meet a systems engineer who wants your help to find a way to use magnets to figure out which boxes are heavy.

Like a systems engineer, you complete activities and labs to learn about factors that affect electric force and magnetic force. You will use what you learn in the lessons to build a device that uses magnetic force to sort objects by weight. Then, you will demonstrate your device and make suggestions to improve it.

Find your Quest activities on pages 52–53, 64, 72–73, 76

Career Connection Systems Engineer page 77

- ▶ **VIDEO**
- 📖 **eTEXT**
- 👆 **INTERACTIVITY**
- 🎚 **VIRTUAL LAB**
- 🎮 **GAME**
- 📄 **DOCUMENT**
- ☑ **ASSESSMENT**

The Essential Question

HANDS-ON LAB

Topic 3
Weather

3-ESS2-1, 3-ESS3-1,
3–5-ETS1-1, 3–5-ETS1-2,
3–5-ETS1-3

 VIDEO

 eTEXT

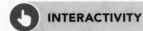 INTERACTIVITY

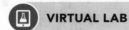 VIRTUAL LAB

 GAME

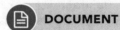 DOCUMENT

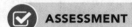 ASSESSMENT

Quest

In this Quest activity, you meet an architect who wants your help to design a wind-resistant roof for a new house.

Like an architect, you complete activities and labs to learn about different weather factors and how they will impact your roof's design. You will use what you learn in the lessons to build different roofs and test how well your models withstand strong winds. Then, you will present your final design for a wind-resistant roof and explain how your roof will protect the house from strong winds.

Find your Quest activities on pages 86–87, 97, 108, 116–117, 118

Career Connection Architect page 119

The Essential Question

HANDS-ON LAB

Climate

Quest

In this Quest activity, you meet a movie location scout who wants your help to choose locations for a new movie. The movie will take place throughout a whole year, but it will be filmed in just a few months. The locations you choose will need to feature different weather.

Like a movie location scout, you complete activities and labs to examine how different types of climate can help you display different types of weather. You will use what you learn in the lessons to identify three outdoor locations for your movie scenes. Then, you will present your research to explain where you want to film and why you chose the locations.

Find your Quest activities on pages 128–129, 140, 148–149, 159,160

Career Connection Movie Location Scout page 161

 VIDEO
 eTEXT
 INTERACTIVITY
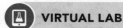 VIRTUAL LAB
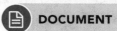 GAME
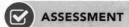 DOCUMENT
 ASSESSMENT

The Essential Question

HANDS-ON LAB

Topic 5

Life Cycles and Traits

3-LS1-1, 3-LS3-1, 3-LS3-2

 VIDEO

 eTEXT

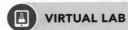 INTERACTIVITY

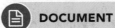 VIRTUAL LAB

 GAME

 DOCUMENT

 ASSESSMENT

Quest

In this Quest activity, you meet an ecologist who wants your help to design plants and animals that would live in a mystery location.

Like an ecologist, you complete activities and labs to evaluate whether different animals would likely survive in different environments. You use what you learn in the lessons to describe what plants or animals would be found in the mystery location.

Find your Quest activities on pages 170–171, 183, 190, 201, 202

Career Connection Ecologist page 203

HANDS-ON LAB

Topic 6

Adaptations and Survival

Quest

In this Quest activity, you meet a conservation biologist who asks you to evaluate the possible effects of construction on a community pond.

Like a conservation biologist, you complete activities and labs to gather information about the interaction of living things and the environment. You use what you learn in the lessons to advise the community about how to reduce possible construction effects on pond organisms.

Find your Quest activities on pages 212–213, 222–223, 230, 241, 244

Career Connection Conservation Biologist page 245

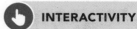 VIDEO

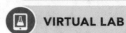 eTEXT

INTERACTIVITY

 VIRTUAL LAB

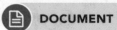 GAME

DOCUMENT

ASSESSMENT

HANDS-ON LAB

Topic 7

Fossil Evidence

Quest

In this Quest activity, you meet a paleontologist who wants your help to figure out where different collected fossils came from.

Like a paleontologist, you complete activities and labs to gather evidence about different fossils and their dig sites. You will use what you learn in the lessons to develop a hypothesis about where the fossils came from. Then, you will write a letter to the paleontologist that uses evidence to explain at which dig site you think each fossil was found.

Find your Quest activities on pages 254–255, 266, 275, 284–285, 286

Career Connection Movie Location Scout page 287

 VIDEO

 eTEXT

 INTERACTIVITY

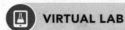 VIRTUAL LAB

 GAME

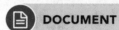 DOCUMENT

 ASSESSMENT

HANDS-ON LAB

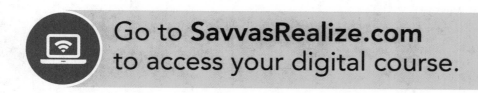

Go to **SavvasRealize.com** to access your digital course.

Elevate Science combines the best science writing with a robust online program. Throughout the lessons, look for digital support to increase your learning experience.

Online Resources

Savvas Realize™ is your online science class. It includes:

- Student eTEXT
- Teacher eTEXT
- Project-Based Learning
- Virtual Labs

- Interactivities
- Videos
- Assessments
- Study Tools
- and more!

Digital Features

 VIDEO

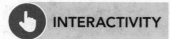 INTERACTIVITY

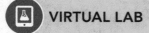 VIRTUAL LAB

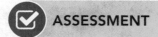 ASSESSMENT

 eTEXT

 GAME

Look for these **symbols**. They tell you that there are more things to do and learn online.

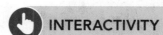 INTERACTIVITY

Complete an interactivity about chemical changes.

Elevate your thinking!

Elevate Science takes science to a whole new level and lets you take ownership of your learning. Explore science in the world around you. Investigate how things work. Think critically and solve problems! *Elevate Science* helps you think like a scientist, so you're ready for a world of discoveries.

Explore Your World

Explore real-life scenarios with engaging Quests that dig into science topics around the world. You can:

- Solve real-world problems
- Apply skills and knowledge
- Communicate solutions

Make Connections

Elevate Science connects science to other subjects and shows you how to better understand the world through:

- Mathematics
- Reading and Writing
- Literacy

Quest Kickoff

STEM Find the Right Mix— and Step on It!

How can we mix ingredients to make a model stepping stone?

Hi, I'm Alicia Gomez, a materials scientist! Suppose a school is setting up a prairie habitat. In this problem-based learning activity, you will build a model stepping stone so that students can observe the habitat without damaging the plants.

Like a materials scientist, you will evaluate your design and learn how different combinations of materials can make your design solution more useful. And you can decorate your model stepping stones, too!

Follow the path to learn how you will complete the Quest. The Quest activities in the lessons will help you complete the Quest! Check off your progress on the path when you com...

Visual Literacy Connection

What is the matter?

All matter is made up of smaller particles. How can you observe the magnification of matter?

If you were to look at a solid object, such as cotton shirt closely, describe what you might observe with your unaided eye?

Sample answers: I might be able to see strands of threads.

Properties of Matter

Build Skills for the Future

- Master the Engineering Design Process
- Apply critical thinking and analytical skills
- Learn about STEM careers

Do you want to be the one who designs an even better surfboard foam? Visit the Career Center to learn about a career as a chemical engineer.

Focus on Reading Skills

Elevate Science creates ongoing reading connections to help you develop the reading skills you need to succeed. Features include:

- Leveled Readers
- Literacy Connection Features
- Reading Checks

Literacy ▸ Toolbox

Use Evidence from Text
Water is formed by the combination of atoms of two different elements— hydrogen and o... smallest partic... atom or a mole... you think so?

☑ READING CHECK **Use Evidence from Text** Why do you think aerogels could be used to clean up oil spills in your community? Underline the important facts from the text that support your claim with evidence.

Enter the Lab

Hands-on experiments and virtual labs help you test ideas and show what you know in performance-based assessments. Scaffolded labs include:

- STEM Labs
- Design Your Own
- Open-ended Labs

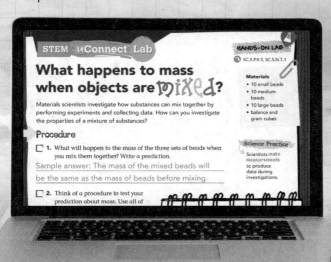

Motion and Forces

Next Generation Science Standards

3-PS2-1 Plan and conduct an investigation to provide evidence of the effects of balanced and unbalanced forces on the motion of an object.

3-PS2-2 Make observations and/or measurements of an object's motion to provide evidence that a pattern can be used to predict future motion.

The Essential Question

How do forces on an object affect its motion?

Show What You Know

What forces are acting on this person?

_____

_____

_____

STEM Pinball Wizard!

How can you use different types of forces to design a pinball machine?

Phenomenon Hi there! My name is Andrew Platt. I am designing a new pinball game for a contest. The object of the game is to collect points while you keep the ball from rolling off the surface. I need your help to design the new game.

In this problem-based learning activity, you will learn how designers use different forces to cause the ball to move in different ways.

Follow the path to learn how you will complete the Quest. The Quest activities in the lessons will help you complete the Quest! Check off your progress on the path when you complete an activity with a QUEST CHECK ✓ OFF. Go online for more Quest activities.

Quest Check-In 1

Lesson 1
Learn about how objects move. Understand how you can get your pinball rolling.

Next Generation Science Standards

3-PS2-1 Plan and conduct an investigation to provide evidence of the effects of balanced and unbalanced forces on the motion of an object.

3-PS2-2 Make observations and/or measurements of an object's motion to provide evidence that a pattern can be used to predict future motion.

Quest Check-In 3

Lesson 3
Discover how to use forces to change motion. Design a system to launch your pinball.

VIDEO

Watch a video about a game designer.

Quest Check-In Lab 4

Lesson 4
Explain how balanced and unbalanced forces affect objects. Model how you can stop your pinball from rolling.

Quest Check-In 2

Lesson 2
Recognize patterns in motion. Design a part of your pinball machine that will cause the ball to move in a predictable way.

Quest Findings

Use what you've learned to design a pinball game! Predict how the ball will move in different parts of your game.

How do things move?

Game designers must understand what causes objects to move in different ways. How can objects made of the same material move differently?

Materials
- sheets of paper
- meterstick
- stopwatch

Procedure

☐ **1.** Drop a sheet of paper from a height of 1 meter. Use the stopwatch to measure how long it takes for the paper to reach the ground. Repeat this step 3 times. Record your observations each time.

☐ **2.** Design a plan to make the paper fall faster or slower. Show your plan to your teacher before you begin.

Science Practice

Scientists use observations and measurements from investigations to explain phenomena.

Analyze and Interpret Data

3. Explain How did the changes you made to the paper affect how quickly it fell? Why do you think this is so?

_____

_____

_____

_____

Observations

4. Predict Based on your observations, would a larger sheet of paper take more or less time to reach the ground?

_____

_____

_____

Draw Conclusions

When you draw conclusions, you use what you know to figure out something that is not stated. Here is how to draw conclusions.

 GAME

Practice what you learn with the Mini Games.

- Identify the important information in the text.

- Think about what you already know about the subject.

- Decide what is likely to be true because of the information.

Read the text about a train engineer.

All Aboard!

Michio is a train engineer. He is the person who drives the train. At first, the train begins to roll slowly down the track. The train goes faster as Michio gives the engine more fuel. Finally, the train hits top speed. It will not take long to reach the train station at this rate.

As the train gets closer to the train station, the train begins to slow. The closer the train gets to its stop, the slower it goes. That is all right, though. The train was going very fast before. The train made it to its stop in good time.

✓ **READING CHECK** Draw Conclusions

When did the train travel the farthest in one minute? Explain how you know.

_____

_____

_____

Motion

I can...

Observe and measure an object's motion.

3-PS2-1

Literacy Skill
Draw Conclusions

Vocabulary
position
direction
motion
distance
speed

Academic Vocabulary
relative

▶ **VIDEO**

Watch a video about position, motion, and speed.

ENGINEERING › Connection

Have you ever ridden on a train without wheels or an engine? In some parts of the world, trains without wheels are already running! These trains are called maglev trains. Powerful magnets cause the trains to float above a "track." The magnets also make the train move forward. The maglev train travels much faster than a regular train—but not as fast as an airplane. Engineers hope that in the future, the maglev train will be able to move faster than an airplane. The first train ever to use this system was in England. Today, maglev trains operate in Japan, South Korea, and China. Would you like to ride one someday?

📓 **Write About It** Do you think that building a maglev train in your area would be a good idea? Why or why not?

How *fast* can it move?

Scientists take careful measurements to understand how objects move. How can you collect data to measure how fast an object travels and if it always travels at the same rate?

Materials
- wind-up toy
- golf ball
- meterstick
- stopwatch
- masking tape

Procedure

☐ **1.** Make a plan to measure how fast the wind-up toy and the golf ball are moving. Make sure to use all of the materials in your plan. Include how you will know how fast the objects are traveling. Show your plan to your teacher before you begin.

☐ **2.** Repeat your plan several times for the wind-up toy and the golf ball. Record your observations each time.

Science Practice

Scientists use observations and measurements from investigations to explain phenomena.

Analyze and Interpret Data

3. CCC Patterns What pattern did you notice for the wind-up toy and the golf ball? Explain.

_____

_____

_____

_____

4. CCC Patterns How can this pattern help you predict the motion of objects in the future? Explain.

_____

_____

Observations

Literacy ▸ Toolbox

Draw Conclusions When you draw conclusions, you use what you know to figure out something. Read the position and motion section. What are some ways that motion can be measured and described?

Look around and you will see many different objects. Each object has a position. The **position** of an object is the exact place where it is. The place where you are right now is your position. Some words that you can use to describe position are *to the right of, behind,* or *above.* Now turn around. Did your position change? Not if you are standing in the exact same place. When you turn around, your direction changes. **Direction** is the way an object faces, such as north, south, or toward the window.

Look at the positions of the blue car and the red car. You can describe the position of the blue car using the position of the red car. Your might say that the blue car is "12 meters behind the red car." As long as the blue car stays the same distance behind the red car, the blue car's relative position does not change. **Relative** means "compared to." Relative position is the position of one object compared with the position of another object. In this case, the other object is the red car.

Describe What is the relative position of the red car?

_____

_____

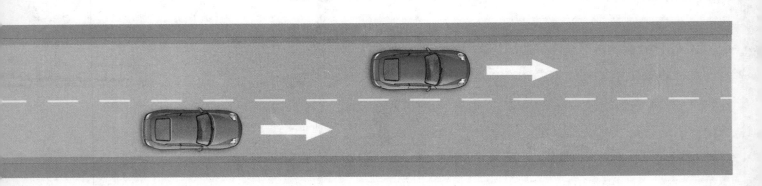

Relative Motion

If the blue car passes the red car, its relative position changes. Now the relative position of the blue car is in front of the red car. Any time an object's position changes, **motion** has happened. The change in an object's position compared to another object's position is its relative motion.

For example, what if you are riding in the blue car? You will pass trees, signs, or buildings that are along the road. You can tell that you are moving if you compare your position to these objects. But what if you compare your position to the position of a friend sitting beside you? Your position relative to the friend does not change.

Apply Describe the motion of the ball relative to the boy.

_____

_____

Model It!

Draw a picture of the moving ball. Also draw a person who would decribe the motion of the ball as toward the left.

Quest Connection

Many games involve the motion of balls. What are some ways that you can get a the direction of a ball to change?

_____

_____

which road is FASTER?

Suppose two families are going to a carnival and want to take the fastest road. How can the families determine which route is the fastest? **Distance** is how far something travels. **Speed** is a measure of how slow or fast something can move. Speed is written as distance per unit of time, such as kilometers per hour.

The family in the **blue car** thinks it will be quicker to take the dirt road. How far do they have to go?

! _____ **kilometers.**

Start

20 km

12:00 pm

The family in the **red car** thinks the highway will be quicker. How far do they have to go?

! _____ **kilometers.**

12:00 pm

Start

20 km

Interpret The red car made it to the carnival first! Explain how the red car made it to the carnival before the blue car.

_____

_____

_____

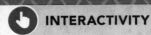
Complete an activity about motion.

Changes in Speed

The man and his dog in the picture are not changing how fast or slow they move across this street. They are moving at a constant speed. They change position at the same rate all the way across the street. But as they continue their walk to the next intersection, they might slow down. They might also move faster. Their speed changes as they move.

☑ **Reading Check** **Draw Conclusions** When you walk down the hallways at school do you change your speed or is your speed constant?

_____

_____

_____

☑ Lesson 1 Check

1. **Vocabulary** How can you measure the motion of an object?

_____

_____

_____

2. **Evaluate** Ball A travels 10 meters in 2 seconds. Ball B travels 30 meters in 10 seconds. How far did each ball go in 1 second? Which ball had the greater speed? Explain your answer.

A when't farther then B

_____

_____

Get Rolling!

Pinball machines are all about movement. To get the game started, players launch the ball up a lane. To launch the ball, the player pulls back on a handle that is connected to a spring. Then they let go of the handle. The farther back the handle is pulled, the harder the ball gets hit.

Look at the diagram of the pinball machine. Do you see the shooting lane? How do you think the ball will travel? Draw a line to trace the path the ball will take after it is launched.

Predict Will the ball always follow the same path?

_____

Explain How could you change the motion of the ball?

_____

_____

_____

_____

_____

_____

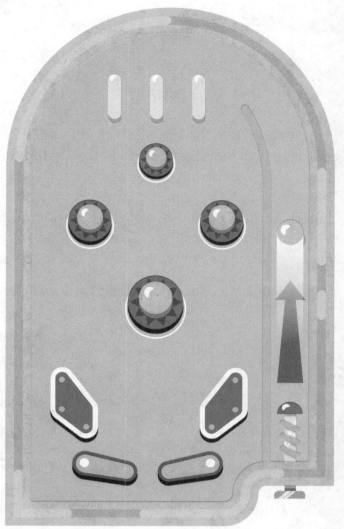

uEngineer It! Build STEM

▶ **INTERACTIVITY**

Go online to learn about other forces involved in transportation.

Riding Above the Lake

Phenomenon The Lake Pontchartrain Causeway in southeastern Louisiana is the longest bridge in the United States. In fact, the causeway is two bridges that run side by side. Each bridge is almost 38.5 kilometers (24 miles) long! They are the largest bridges over a body of water in the United States. The causeway allows people to get across the lake quickly. Without the causeway, people would have to drive around the lake. If you rely on bridges to get where you're going, be sure to thank an engineer!

Would you like to design amazing bridges?

Build It

Suppose you are an engineer. You have been brought onto a small island to connect it to another small island. Only one island has a school. If the islands are connected, children on both islands can go to school. You must build a bridge made out of only three materials that are found on the island.

☐ Choose three materials to build a bridge.

☐ You must build the longest bridge you can in 10 minutes. The bridge should cross the gap between two tables.

☐ Use your choice of materials to fill in the table below.

Materials	Reason for choosing materials

☐ Make a plan to build your bridge. Show your plan to your teacher before you begin.

☐ Build your bridge!

Patterns in Motion

Use patterns to predict future motion.
3-PS2-2

Literacy Skill
Draw Conclusions

Academic Vocabulary
predict

▶ **VIDEO**

Watch a video about patterns in motion.

SPORTS Connection

Figure skating is a sport in which ice-skaters move in patterns on ice. They do jumps, spins, lifts, and other movements. Sometimes they move slowly. Other times they spin fast.

Figure skaters use science to control their spins. When this figure skater holds her arms out wide, her spin will be slow. As she draws her arms in closer to her body, the spin will be faster. She will also spin fast with her arms straight up in the air. To slow down again, all she must do is hold her arms out again.

Identify In what other sports can you observe a spinning motion?

_____

_____

How can you describe the motion of an object?

Scientists investigate patterns to predict the motion of objects. How can you predict how objects will move?

Materials
- large plastic bowl
- two balls with different masses

Science Practice

Scientists carry out investigations to find patterns in the natural world.

Procedure

☐ **1.** Place the bowl on a table. Hold the lighter ball inside the bowl at the top. Let go of the ball. Observe its motion.

☐ **2.** Predict if the other ball will move the same way.

_____

_____

☐ **3. SEP Plan and Conduct an Investigation** Make a plan to test your prediction. Show your plan to your teacher before you begin. Record your observations.

Analyze and Interpret Data

4. CCC Patterns What patterns did you observe during your investigation?

_____

_____

_____

_____

5. Identify Use the pattern to predict how an even heavier ball will move.

_____

Observations

Patterns of Motion

Many types of motion can be described by patterns. You can observe and identify the pattern of a swing as it moves back and forth in the breeze. You can use what you observe about the motion of the swing to predict how it will move. When you **predict**, you tell what will happen in the future. Understanding how objects move and why they move that way will help you predict how an object will move.

Sometimes the pattern of a motion is easy to see. A seesaw goes up and down. A ball rolls in a straight line if you give it a push. But if you drop the ball, it bounces. Other patterns of motion are harder to see. The sound speakers on a TV vibrate, or move back and forth. We cannot see those vibrations.

Predict What will happen if you bounce this ball? Draw arrows to show the pattern of the moving ball.

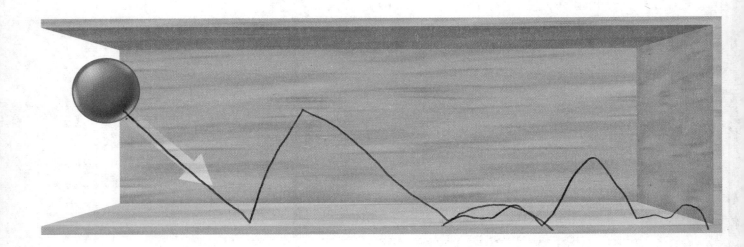

Changing Motion

If a strong wind blows, a wind chime will swing back and forth quickly. If the wind stops, the wind chime will swing more slowly until it stops. When a mild breeze blows, the chime will not move as quickly as it does when the strong wind blows. If the wind changes direction, the chime will move in different directions. The pattern of the wind chime's movement will also change.

Describe Identify another object that moves in a pattern. Describe the pattern of its movement.

_____

_____

_____

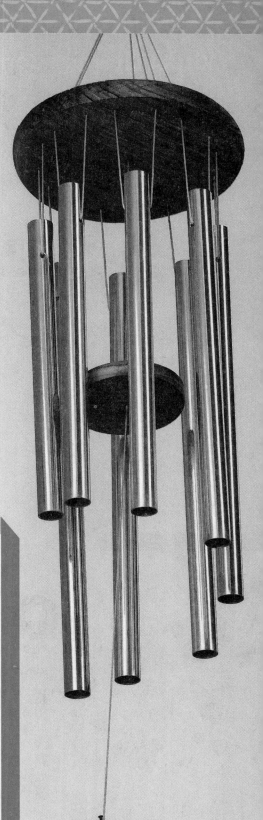

Quest Connection

To play a game with a ball, players should be able to predict where the ball will go when they do certain things to it. What are some things you can do to a ball to make it move in a certain way?

_____

_____

_____

How high can it fly?

Height: 7.5 meters above ground

The circus is in town! People are excited to see trapeze artists fly through the air. Before the show, the technicians test the equipment to make sure it is safe.

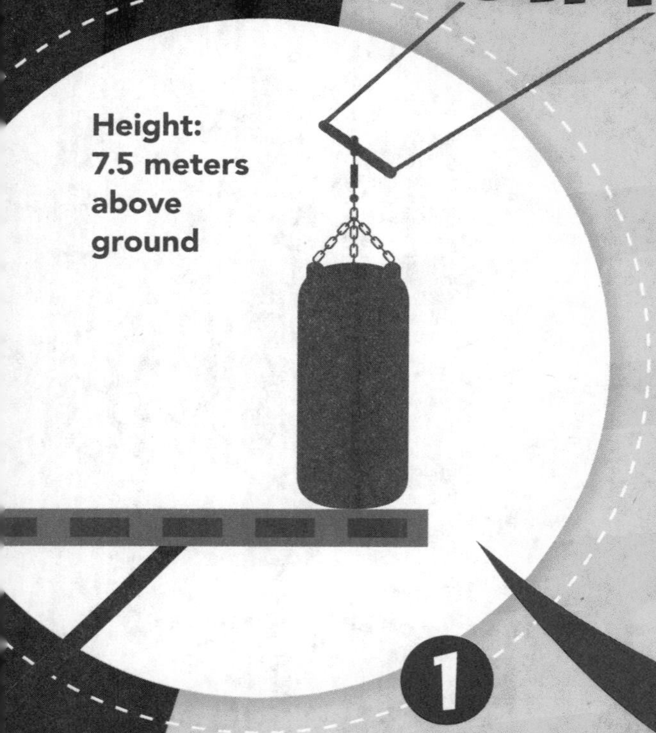

1

The trapeze does **not move** yet. A weight hangs on the bar and is ready to swing.

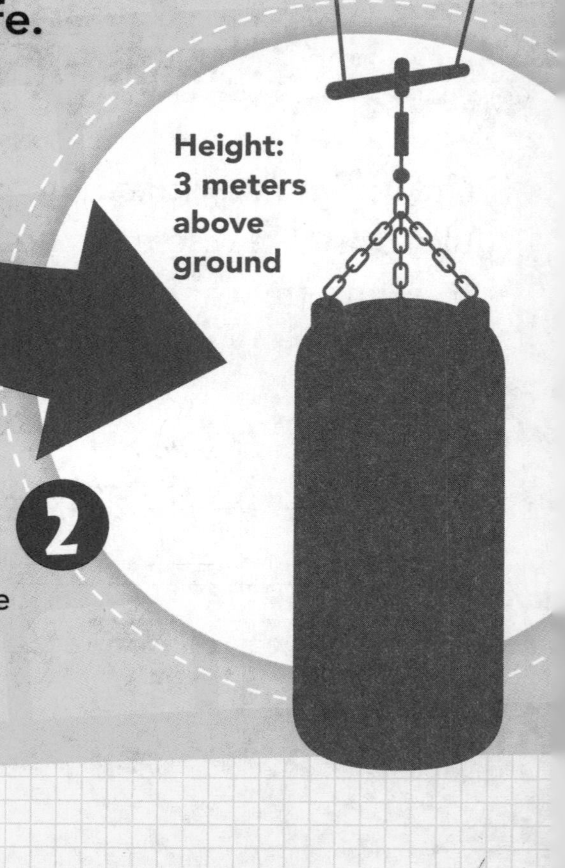

Height: 3 meters above ground

2

With the greatest of ease, the trapeze flies through the air! It really **moves fast** now.

Bouncing Around Ideas

The handle of a pinball machine is pulled back and let go. The pinball goes up the shooting lane. Then it comes back down the table in another part of the machine. If that was all it did, though, the game would be pretty boring! In a good pinball game, you can make the ball move how you want it to.

Two features of pinball machines are flippers and bumpers. You cannot move bumpers. The ball just bounces off them. You can move the flippers back and forth by pushing the buttons on the side of the machine.

Draw a picture of what the bumpers and flippers will look like in your game. Use arrows to indicate how you think these features will make the ball move.

Forces and Motion

I can...

Identify the forces acting on an object.

3-PS2-1

Literacy Skill
Draw Conclusions

Vocabulary
force
contact forces
tension force
spring force
friction
noncontact forces
gravity

Academic Vocabulary
exert

▶ **VIDEO**

Watch a video about forces and motion.

STEM Connection

In the late 1800s, an engineer named Moses Crane saw a problem with the game of football. He could not see the football during a game. So, he used his engineering skills to invent a new game. The new game was called pushball. It was played on the same field that football was played on. But the ball was about 2 meters wide and weighed about 22 kilograms! He thought that changes to the size and shape of the ball would make seeing the ball easier. Crane also wanted to make the game more of a team effort. He certainly succeeded at both of his goals.

📓 **Write About It** What kinds of engineering skills did Moses Crane need to use to design pushball? How could you use similar skills to design a new game?

What makes it move?

Scientists plan investigations to understand how objects move. What are some ways to make a ball move?

Materials
- steel ball

Suggested Materials
- magnet
- meterstick
- straw

Procedure

☐ 1. **SEP Plan an Investigation** Choose three materials that you will use to make the ball move.

☐ 2. Make a plan to use each material to move the ball.

☐ 3. Show your plan to your teacher before you begin. Record your observations.

Science Practice

Scientists plan and carry out investigations to answer a scientific question.

What I did	How the ball moved

Analyze and Interpret Data

4. **CCC Cause and Effect** How could you make the ball move faster with each material?

_____

_____

_____

Cause and Effect Describe
a pattern in motion you use
to make predictions.

Forces

A **force** is a push or a pull. When you pull up a zipper, you **exert**, or apply, a force to the zipper. You pull on the zipper, and the zipper changes its position. A force can start or stop the motion of an object. It can change the direction that an object is moving. A force can also speed up or slow down a moving object.

Suppose only one dog pulled the sled in the photo. The dog would exert a force on the sled. The sled would move forward at a certain speed. If more than one dog pulled on the sled, the sled would move faster. The strength of the force is greater when more dogs are pulling. So, if the force that acts on an object is greater, so is its change in motion.

Describe Suppose you are pushing a friend on a sled. How could you speed up or slow down the sled?

_____

_____

_____

Contact Forces

When you sit on a chair, you exert a force on the chair. The force pushes downward on the chair. The chair also pushes upward on you! The force that you and the chair exert are contact forces. **Contact forces** act between objects that are touching.

You observe many kinds of contact forces every day. **Tension force** is a pulling force that stretches something. The girl in the photo is exerting a tension force on the yellow band. At the same time, the yellow band is exerting a spring force on the girl. **Spring force** is exerted by an object that has been stretched or squeezed. When the girl lets go of the stretched band, it will snap back to its original position. **Friction** is a force that goes against the motion of an object. When the bike moves over the road, its wheels rub against the road. The force of friction will slow the bike if the rider does not continue to push on the pedals.

Identify Give another example of each of the three kinds of contact forces.

_____

_____

_____

_____

_____

uBe a Scientist

Friction
How does the kind of surface affect friction? Rub an object over a smooth surface. Then rub the same object over a rough surface. On which surface can you move the object more easily?

tension force and spring force

friction force

what are noncontact forces?

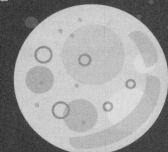

Some forces can cause a push or a pull on an object without touching it. Forces that can act at a distance are called **noncontact forces**. Three types of noncontact forces are gravity, electricity, and magnetism.

Gravity

Gravity is a **force** that acts between any two objects that pulls them toward one another. Draw arrows to show the direction of the gravitational forces between the following:

• Earth and the satellite
• Earth and the moon

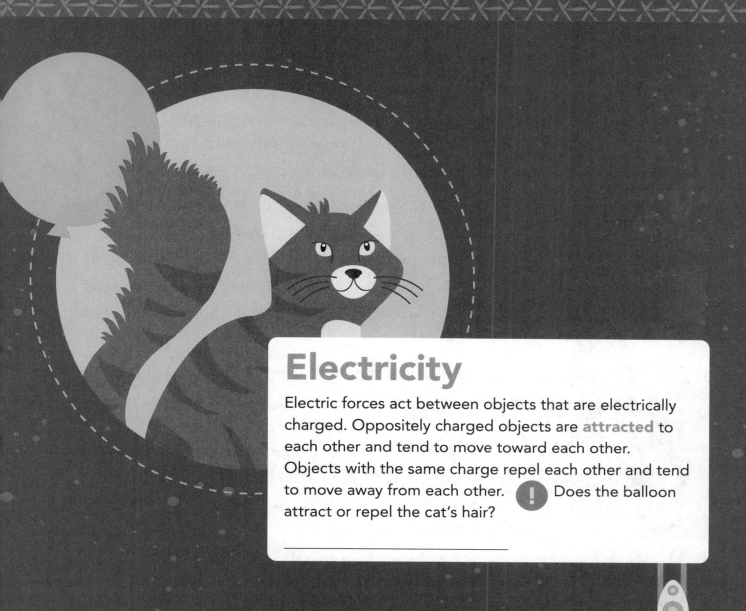

Electricity

Electric forces act between objects that are electrically charged. Oppositely charged objects are **attracted** to each other and tend to move toward each other. Objects with the same charge repel each other and tend to move away from each other. ❗ Does the balloon attract or repel the cat's hair?

_____

Magnetism

Magnetic force is a noncontact force that can **exert a pull** on magnetic objects, such as iron. Magnets can either attract or repel other magnets. Draw an arrow to show the direction of the force that the magnet is exerting.

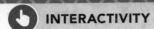

Equal and Opposite Forces

You have read about pairs of forces, such as those that act when you sit on a chair. You push downward on the chair, and the chair pushes upward on you.

Because neither motion is changing, we say that the forces are equal and opposite. The strength of your downward force is the same as the strength of the chair's upward force on you. Forces that are equal and opposite do not cause a change in motion.

Another example is when a soccer ball is kicked at the same time with equal but opposite forces by two players. The forces are the same but opposite, so the ball has no change in motion. So what must happen for the forces to make the ball move? To make the ball move, the forces must be unbalanced. They must not be equal and opposite. You can make the forces unbalanced by having one player kick the ball harder. Forces that are not balanced cause a change in motion.

Quest Connection

What are some ways you can change the motion of a moving pinball?

_____

_____

Combined Forces

Many forces can act on an object at the same time. Think about the forces that act when you ride a bike. Your feet push on the pedals to make the bike move forward. Friction acts on the bike wheels to slow the bike. You push harder on one side of your handlebars to turn the bike. Each force has its own strength. But the forces combine to keep the bike moving.

☑ READING CHECK Draw Conclusions What conclusions can you make about the contact forces that are acting on a moving bike?

_____

_____

☑ Lesson 3 Check

1. **Compare and Contrast** How are the forces of friction and gravity alike? How are they different?

_____

_____

_____

_____

2. **Apply** Identify the forces that are acting on a boy who is being pulled by a dog on a leash.

_____

_____

_____

Launch Your Pinball!

One important part of your pinball game will be the launcher. It gets the ball moving without you touching the ball with your hands. The launcher has to be strong enough to exert a force on the ball to make it go, but it cannot be too strong, or you might break your pinball machine! Draw your design.

Will your design be able to apply enough force to the pinball? What can you do to make sure that it will work?

_____

_____

_____

Multiply and Divide

A gear is a simple machine that uses contact forces. It is a wheel with edges that stick out, called cogs. The cogs of one gear fit inside, or mesh with, cogs on other gears. If one gear turns, it makes the other gears it meshes with turn also. The gears turn one cog at a time. They will turn faster or slower depending on how many cogs they have. Here is an example: A gear with 10 cogs is turning a gear with 5 cogs. Since $10 \div 5 = 2$, the gear with 5 cogs will spin twice as fast. Use multiplication and division to find the relative speed of these gears.

The gear with 30 cogs spins 20 times per minute. How many times will the gear with 15 cogs turn in a minute?

_____

_____

The gear with 24 cogs turns 20 times per minute. How many times will the gear with 8 cogs turn in a minute?

_____

_____

_____

_____

Balanced and Unbalanced Forces

I can...

Use evidence to explain how balanced and unbalanced forces affect an object's motion.

3-PS2-1

Literacy Skill
Draw Conclusions

Vocabulary
balanced forces
net force

Academic Vocabulary
equation

▶ **VIDEO**

Watch a video about unbalanced forces.

CURRICULUM › Connection

Have you ever taken an elevator to the top of a very tall building? If so, then you should thank an engineer named Elisha Otis. He did not invent the first elevator. He did make them much safer to use, though. The first elevators were simple—and dangerous! Each elevator had just one cable to raise and lower it. If tension force caused the cable to snap, the elevator would fall very quickly. Elisha Otis used his engineering skills to design a brake to stop the elevator. The tension on the cable would keep a spring stretched. If the cable broke, the spring would snap back to its original shape. This action caused a brake to stop the elevator. The Otis elevator helped people design safer and taller buildings.

☑ **READING CHECK** **Draw Conclusions**
What force would cause an elevator to fall?

How can you hold up an object?

Engineers use forces to build structures that are safe. How can you balance forces to build a structure that can safely hold a steel ball?

Materials
• steel ball
• safety goggles

Suggested Materials
• string
• wooden sticks
• magnets
• building blocks

Design and Build

☐ 1. **SEP Plan an Investigation** Choose materials to build a structure. Draw the design for your structure. Add labels to show how the materials will be used.

☐ 2. **SEP Carry Out an Investigation** Show your design to your teacher before you start building.

⚠ Wear safety goggles.

⚠ Be careful handling materials.

Engineering Practice

Engineers use models to analyze a system.

Evaluate Your Design

3. **Evaluate** What forces did your design try to balance?

_____

_____

4. **Assess** How could your design be improved?

_____

_____

How can you move an object?

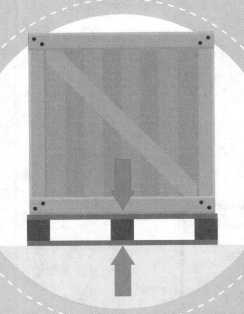

1

Gravity is pulling downward on the crate. The ground is pushing the crate up. When both forces are equally strong, the forces are called **balanced forces**. The arrows are the same length. This shows two opposite forces of equal strength.

2

The machine is pulling the crate, but it is not yet moving.

⚠ What force balances the machine's pull?

_____

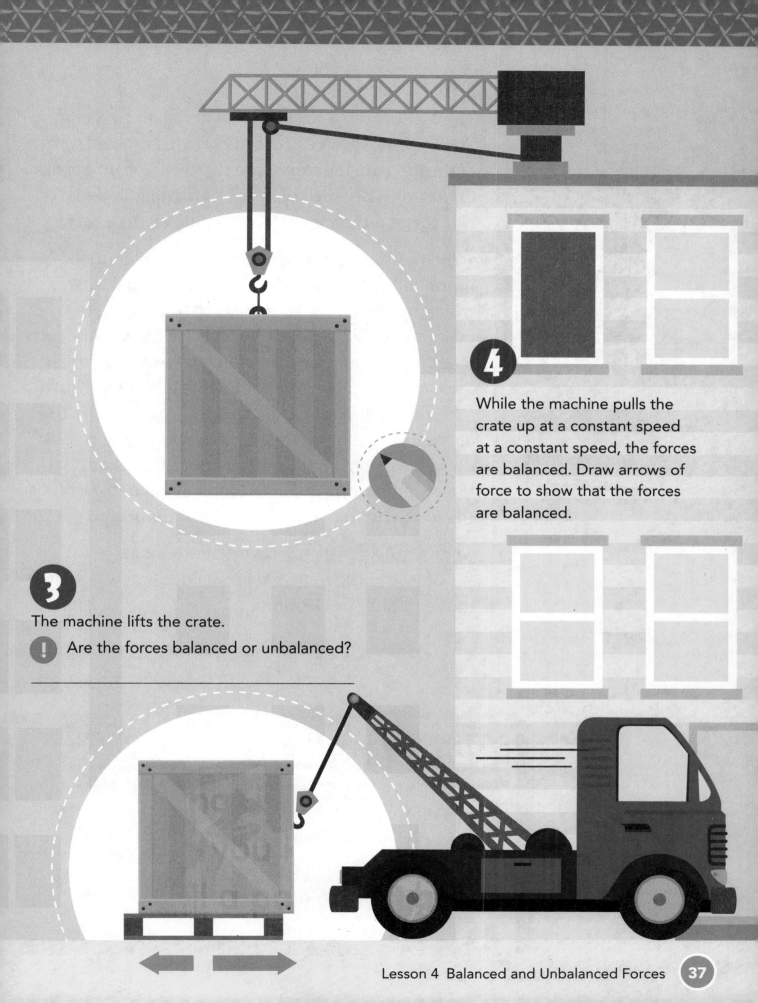

4

While the machine pulls the crate up at a constant speed at a constant speed, the forces are balanced. Draw arrows of force to show that the forces are balanced.

3

The machine lifts the crate.

! Are the forces balanced or unbalanced?

_____

Net Force

Think about a piano being held in the air by a crane. The downward force of gravity and the upward force of the rope are the same. The two forces act in opposite directions. They are balanced, so their net force is 0. **Net force** is the sum of forces acting on an object.

You can use an **equation**, or math problem, to figure out net force. Force is measured in a unit called newtons (N). You and a friend are each pushing on a box with a force of 1 N. If you are both pushing in the same direction, you are applying a force of 1 N + 1 N. Your net force is 2 N. If you push in opposite directions, each of your pushes is still equal to 1 N. But because you are going in opposite directions, you would subtract the forces. Your net force would be 0. When net force is equal to 0, all of the forces acting on an object are balanced.

✓ READING CHECK Draw Conclusions
What would the net force on the nonmoving piano in the picture be? Explain.

_____

_____

Quest Connection

Describe how you can use forces to change the motion of the moving ball in your pinball machine.

_____

_____

Measuring Forces

How can you find the strength of a force? You can use a spring scale. An object attached to the spring scale exerts a tension force. A scale measures that tension. If no tension acts on the spring scale, its spring will not stretch. The scale will show a net force of 0 N. The greater the tension on the spring, the more the spring will stretch. As a spring stretches farther, the applied force becomes greater.

Explain What is the strength of the spring's force acting on the apple? How do you know?

_____

_____

_____

☑ Lesson 4 Check

1. **Apply Concepts** A box is resting on a table. Gravity pulls the box downward with a force of 25 N. With how much force is the table pushing upward on the box?

   _____

2. **Vocabulary** Use the terms *balanced* and *net force* to describe the forces acting on the box.

   _____

   _____

   _____

How can you control your flippers?

One part of any pinball machine is the flippers. How much force must the paddles exert to stop or change the motion of the ball?

Materials
- steel ball
- safety goggles

Suggested Materials
- craft sticks
- hole punch
- paper fasteners
- spring scale
- blocks
- cardboard
- books

Design and Build

☐ **1.** What criteria must the flippers meet to change the motion of the pinball?

_____

_____

_____

 Wear safety goggles.

Engineering Practice

Engineers use models to predict how systems will respond to variables.

☐ **2. SEP Develop Models** Draw a model you can use to see whether the flippers can change the motion of the ball. Choose materials you want to use for your design.

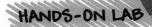
☐ **3. SEP Use Models** Make a plan to build and test your model. Show your plan to your teacher before you build your model. Test it.

Evaluate Your Design

4. CCC Cause and Effect How were the flippers able to change the motion of the ball?

_____

_____

_____

_____

5. SEP Evaluate Information Compare your model with the models of other students. What design features made paddles more successful than others? Which, if any, of these features could make your model better?

_____

_____

_____

_____

_____

INTERACTIVITY

Organize data to support your Quest Findings.

STEM ▶ Pinball Wizard!

How can you use different types of forces to design a pinball machine?

Phenomenon The deadline has finally arrived! It is time to submit your design for your pinball machine. Draw the design for your new pinball machine. Be sure to label all of the important parts. Draw arrows that show the direction the ball will most likely move at different places on the game table. Make sure you have fun with your design, too, by making it colorful and creative!

pinball arcade

2. Identify Variables What does the Y arrow in the diagram represent?

A. the force of gravity

B. the force of friction

C. Mike's falling motion

D. the speed of falling snow

3. Evaluate Mike begins to push with his ski poles, but he does not move. Which of these choices explains why?

A. The force of gravity is holding Mike on Earth's surface.

B. The force of friction is stronger than the force of Mike's push.

C. The force of gravity is balanced by the force of the hill pushing up.

D. The force of Mike's push is unbalanced because of the wind's force.

4. Patterns Mike pushes a little harder and starts moving down the hill. Write a prediction about what will happen to Mike's motion and why it will happen.

_____

_____

_____

_____

Why do objects move?

Phenomenon Scientists investigate how matter acts so they can predict future events. How can you investigate how objects can begin moving?

Plan Your Procedure

☐ **1.** Prop one end of the cardboard on a book. Use the protractor to measure the angle between the cardboard and the surface it is resting on. Place an object at the high end of the cardboard.

☐ **2.** Let go of the object and observe whether it moves down the cardboard. Record your data.

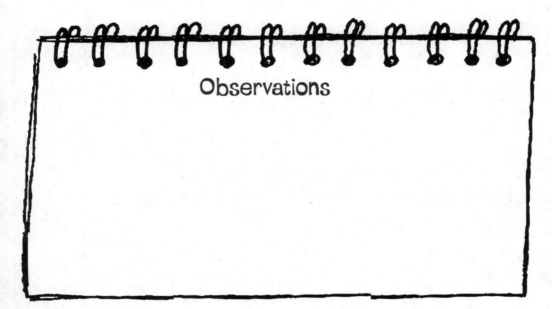

Observations

☐ **3.** Make a plan to make an object move down the cardboard. Show your plan to your teacher before you begin.

_____

_____

_____

Materials

- objects of different masses
- heavy cardboard
- books
- balance
- gram cubes
- plastic protractor

Science Practice

Scientists use observations and measurements from investigations to explain phenomena.

☐ **4.** Predict whether objects of different masses will move in the same way.

_____

_____

☐ **5.** Write a plan to test your prediction.

_____

_____

_____

_____

_____

Evaluate Your Plan

6. Identify What forces acted on the objects while they were on the ramp?

_____

_____

7. Draw Conclusions How did the forces change as you conducted your investigation?

_____

_____

_____

_____

_____

Electricity and Magnetism

Lesson 1 Electric Forces

Lesson 2 Magnetic Forces

Next Generation Science Standards

3-PS2-3 Ask questions to determine cause and effect relationships of electric or magnetic interactions between two objects not in contact with each other.

3-PS2-4 Define a simple design problem that can be solved by applying scientific ideas about magnets.

3-5-ETS1-1 Define a simple design problem reflecting a need or a need or a want that includes specified criteria for success and constraints on materials, time, or cost.

Go online to access
your digital course.

▶ VIDEO

📖 eTEXT

👆 INTERACTIVITY

📱 VIRTUAL LAB

🎮 GAME

☑ ASSESSMENT

The Essential Question

How can you solve a problem using magnetic forces?

Show What You Know

This large magnet lifts scrap and then drops it in a truck.
What kind of material can the magnet pick up?

_____

_____

Weigh to Go

How can you use magnets to save time?

Phenomenon Hi! I am Elaine Plank, a systems engineer. I solve problems to make systems work better. The packing system in a warehouse needs to identify how boxes will be shipped. Heavy boxes go to one truck. Lighter boxes go to another truck. It takes workers a lot of time to weigh each box.

In this problem-based learning activity, you will help find a way to use magnets to figure out which boxes are heavy.

The Quest activities in each lesson will guide you through your design process. As you complete each part of the Quest, use a QUEST CHECK ✓ OFF to mark your progress. Go online for more Quest activities.

Quest Check-In 1

Lesson 1
Learn about factors that affect electric force.

Next Generation Science Standards

3-PS2-4 Define a simple design problem that can be solved by applying scientific ideas about magnets.

3-5-ETS1-1 Define a simple design problem reflecting a need or a need or a want that includes specified criteria for success and constraints on materials, time, or cost.

Quest Check-In Lab 2

Lesson 2

Build a device that uses magnetic force to sort objects by weight.

THIS WAY UP

THIS WAY UP

22.6kg

JP

THIS WAY UP

Quest Findings

Demonstrate your device and make suggestions to improve it.

EXPRESS

How can you *move objects* without touching them?

Some forces work on objects without touching them. How can you make an object move without touching it?

Procedure

☐ **1.** Place a balloon next to a wool cloth. Observe what happens. Then rub the balloon with the wool cloth. What happens when you pull the wool cloth away from the balloon?

_____

_____

☐ **2. SEP Ask Questions** Based on the materials available, write a question about moving objects without touching them.

_____

_____

☐ **3. SEP Plan an Investigation** Write a plan to investigate your question. Have your teacher approve your plan. Test your plan. Record your observations.

Analyze and Interpret Data

4. SEP Draw Conclusions What can you conclude from your investigation to answer your question?

_____

_____

Materials
- balloons
- wool cloth
- tissue paper
- foam packing material

Science Practice

Scientists **ask questions** that can be investigated.

Sequence

Literacy Connection

 GAME

Practice what you learn with the Mini Games.

When you sequence things that happen, you tell what happened in the correct order. When you read text, look for words that give clues to a sequence. Look for words such as *first, then,* and *finally.*

Read this paragraph about magnets.

Lode the Way!

People first learned about magnets when they observed that certain rocks pulled some kinds of metal toward them. This rock was called a lodestone. They observed that lodestones could be used to turn an iron needle into a magnet. These iron needles were then used to make compasses. Sailors have used these compasses for a very long time. Engineers have found many uses for magnets in modern machines.

☑ **READING CHECK** **Sequence** Use numbers to show the order of things that happened.

_____ People made needles into magnets.

_____ People use magnets in many ways today.

_____ People used needles for compasses.

_____ People learned that lodestone attracts iron.

Electric Forces

I can...

Relate the causes and effects of electric forces between objects.

3-PS2-3

Literacy Skill
Sequence

Vocabulary
electric charge
neutral
repel
attract
electric force
conductor
insulator
static discharge

Academic Vocabulary
source

 VIDEO

Watch a video about electric forces.

SPORTS ▶ Connection

Swimmers are getting ready for a swim meet. Some clouds are in the sky. But the sun is shining at the swimming pool. Then a lifeguard sees the flash of distant lightning. He blows his whistle loudly. Everyone gets out of the pool right away. They move into the locker room before the storm arrives. Why is there so much concern?

The electricity of lightning can travel very far from the storm. It can strike people and other objects 15 kilometers (10 miles) or more away from where rain is falling. And it can travel through water very easily. People can be seriously hurt if they are struck by lightning. That is why everyone must get out of the water when a thunderstorm is moving to the area of the pool. When you take part in outdoor sports, be very careful of lightning.

☑ **Reading Check Sequence** Underline the sentence in the first paragraph to show what happened first at the swim meet. Circle the sentence that shows what the people did next.

uInvestigate Lab

HANDS-ON LAB

3-PS2-3, SEP.1

How can you keep objects in the air?

Materials
- cloth
- 2 foam plates

Suggested Materials
- PVC pipe
- plastic bag

Scientists investigate how forces interact to cause changes. How can you use forces to keep an object in the air without touching it?

Procedure

☐ **1.** Rub the cloth on one foam plate. Try to place the other plate on top of it. Observe what happens.

☐ **2.** Write a question about keeping objects in the air that you could investigate using the materials.

Science Practice

Scientists ask questions about the natural world.

_____

_____

_____

☐ **3.** Plan a way to test your question. Show your plan to your teacher before you begin. Record your observations.

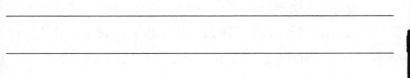

Observations

Analyze and Interpret Data

4. Infer What can you infer from your observations?

_____

_____

_____

_____

Electric Charge

You walk on a carpet and then touch a doorknob. A small spark jumps between your hand and the doorknob. You hear a crackling sound. You got an electric shock. The overall cause of the shock is a force.

positive

negative

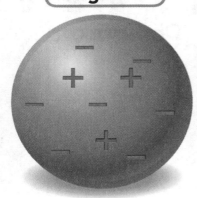

neutral

All matter is made of small particles. One property of these particles is that they can have electric charges. Some charges are positive (+). Other charges are negative (–). When matter has an overall positive charge or a negative charge, we say that it has an **electric charge**.

Some matter has more positive particles than negative particles. We say that the matter has a positive charge. Likewise, if the matter has more negative charges than positive charges, then it has a negative charge. If the number of positive and negative charges are the same, the matter is **neutral**, or has no electric charge.

Evaluate Draw a picture of an object that is neutral.

Attract or Repel

When two objects with electric charge are close to one another, a force happens between them. If both objects have negative electric charges, the two objects **repel**, or push away, each other. The same thing happens if both objects have a positive charge. But if one object has a positive charge and the other has a negative charge, each object **attracts**, or pulls on, the other object. The push or pull of charged objects on each other is an **electric force**.

Recognize Label the balloons to tell whether they will attract or repel each other. Explain why you labeled the balloons this way.

_____

_____

_____

Model It! How would you model two charged objects attracting or repelling each other? Draw your model. Use balls, ramps, and springs in the design of your model.

HOW DO Electric Charges Move?

Electric charges move inside objects. The way they move depends on the kind of material the object is made of. Some materials, such as most metals, are conductors. In a **conductor,** electrical charges can move easily. Other materials, such as a rubber balloon, are insulators. In an **insulator,** electric charges cannot move easily.

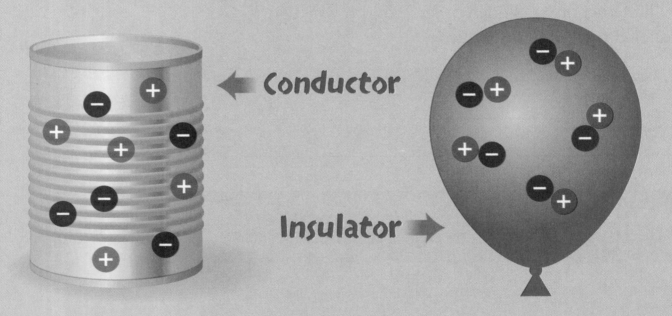

← Conductor

Insulator →

All materials are made up of charged particles. When the number of positive charges and the number of negative charges are the same, the material is neutral.

Neutral

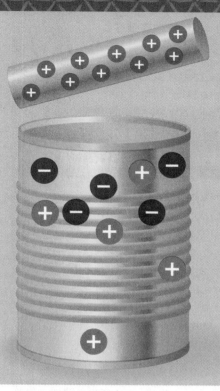

In a conductor, such as a metal can, negative electrical charges can move easily.

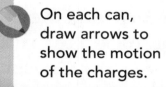 On each can, draw arrows to show the motion of the charges.

When a rod that is negatively charged is close to a conductor, the negative charges of the rod repel the negative charges of the conductor. An electric force causes this motion. The positive charges stay in place.

When a rod that is positively charged is close to a conductor, the negative charges of the conductor are attracted to the positive charges of the rod. They move toward the rod. The positive charges stay in place.

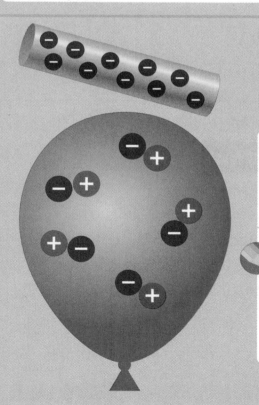

In an insulator, such as a balloon, electric charges cannot move easily.

In the balloon on the right, draw the location of the charges after the charged rod is brought close.

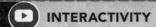
Be a Scientist

Test Electric Charges

Sprinkle a small amount of baby powder or other fine powder on a plate. Run a plastic or rubber comb through your hair several times. Hold the comb close to the powder and observe what happens.

Moving Charges

Sometimes charges can transfer from a charged object to another object—even if the two objects do not touch. **Static discharge** is the transfer of particles that have an electric charge between objects that are not touching. For example, when you walk across some carpets, negatively charged particles in the carpet move to your body. Your body then has a negative electric charge. When your finger comes near a doorknob, the electric force between your finger and the doorknob causes static discharge to occur. When a spark jumps between your finger and a doorknob, a static discharge has happened. A lightning strike is also a static discharge, but it is much more powerful.

✓ **Reading Check** **Sequence** What is the sequence that causes a static discharge when you touch a doorknob?

_____

_____

_____

Quest Connection

▼▼▼▼▼▼▼▼▼▼▼▼▼▼▼▼▼▼▼▼▼▼▼▼▼▼▼▼

Noncontact forces can cause objects to move toward or away from one another. What information do you need to predict which way objects with electric charges will move?

_____

_____

Strength of Electric Force

Two factors affect how strong the electric forces between objects are—the amount of electric charge the objects have and the distance between the objects. Objects with a lot of electric charge will have a greater electric force than objects with less electric charge. The **source**, or cause, of the force is the charge.

The strength of electric force becomes stronger as electrically charged objects get closer to each other. If the objects are farther apart, the force is weaker.

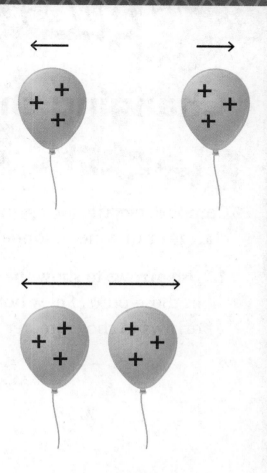

Analyze The arrows above the balloons show the direction of the force on each balloon. Why do you think that the arrows above the bottom balloons are longer than the arrows above the top balloons?

_____

_____

☑ Lesson 1 Check

1. **Identify** What are two ways that you can make the electric forces between two objects stronger?

_____

_____

2. **Predict** A metal rod has a negative electric charge. What will happen if the rod is placed close to a table tennis ball that has a negative electric charge?

_____

_____

Changing the Electric Force

Compare electric forces and how they change when electric charge or distance change.

1. Use arrows to show the electric force acting on each object in these pairs. Show both strength and direction. Use longer arrows to show greater force.

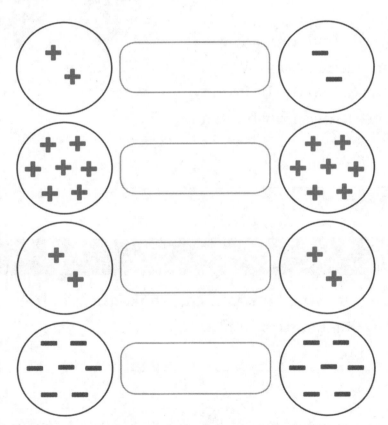

2. How did you decide which arrows should be longer and which arrows should be shorter?

_____

_____

QUEST CHECK ✔ OFF

Find Total Charge

You can find the total charge on an object by comparing the number of positive charges and negative charges. An object that has an equal number of both kinds of charge is neutral. The total charge is zero.

A scientist adds charges to an object and records the data:

Before adding charges	+ + − −
After adding charges	+ + + + + + − − −

What is the total charge on the object after adding charges?

_____positive charges (+) − _____negative charges (−) = _____

Next the scientist doubles the total of both positive and negative charges. Complete the chart to show the change.

Before doubling charges	+ + + + + + − − −
After doubling charges	

What is the total charge on the object after adding charges?

_____ positive charges − _____ negative charges = _____

Lesson 2

Magnetic Forces

I can...

Describe factors that affect magnetic forces between objects.

3-PS2-3, 3-PS2-4, 3-5-ETS1-1

Literacy Skill
Sequence

Vocabulary

natural magnet
permanent magnet
electromagnet
magnetic pole
magnetic field

Academic Vocabulary

interact

 VIDEO

Watch a video about magnetic forces.

CURRICULUM › Connection

Cows sometimes pick up small pieces of metal and swallow them along with their food. Sharp objects can poke through the wall of the stomach and make the cow sick. Farmers often have their cows swallow a long, smooth magnet. In the stomach, the magnet attracts those bits of metal. Since the metal cannot move around much, a problem is less likely. The magnet can protect the cow for many years.

Identify In the paragraph above, circle the kinds of objects that stick to cow magnets.

Magnets

A magnet is an object that attracts certain kinds of metal. A magnet attracts most objects made of iron or steel. Some kinds of rock are natural magnets. A **natural magnet** is not made magnetic by people. The largest natural magnet on Earth is the planet itself.

How can you make a mag∩et?

Engineers use what they know about materials to help solve problems. How can an object become a magnet?

Materials
- magnet
- large metal paper clip
- small metal paper clip

Develop a Solution

☐ **1. SEP Ask Questions** Write a question about how to use the materials to make a magnet.

_____

_____

☐ **2.** Make a plan to answer your question. Include how you will test your solution. Show your plan to your teacher before you begin. Record your observations.

Evaluate Your Solution

3. Identify What criteria did your solution meet?

_____

_____

_____

4. Analyze Were you able to pick up the small paper clip? Why or why not?

_____

_____

_____

Engineering Practice

Engineers solve problems by designing and developing objects.

Observations

How do people use electromagnets?

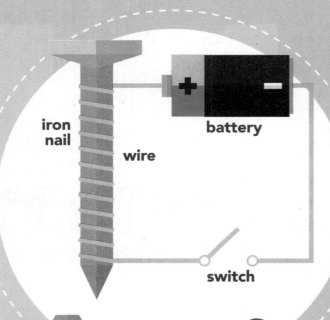

iron nail

wire

battery

switch

Most magnets are **permanent magnets.** Their magnetism cannot be turned on and off. **Electromagnets** are magnets that can be turned on and off by an electric current. When the current is on, the electromagnet attracts magnetic objects. When the current is off, the magnet turns off.

Moving **electric charges** in the wire cause the nail to become a magnet. Compare the two drawings and circle the part of the device that changed.

1

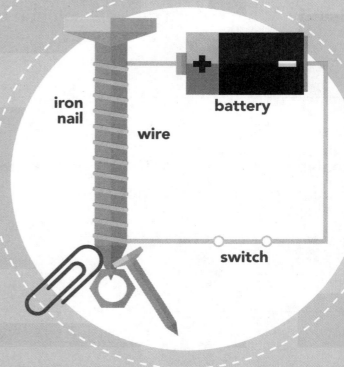

iron nail

wire

battery

switch

When the doorbell switch is on, the magnet turns on. What is the bar connected to the **hammer** made of?

2

_____

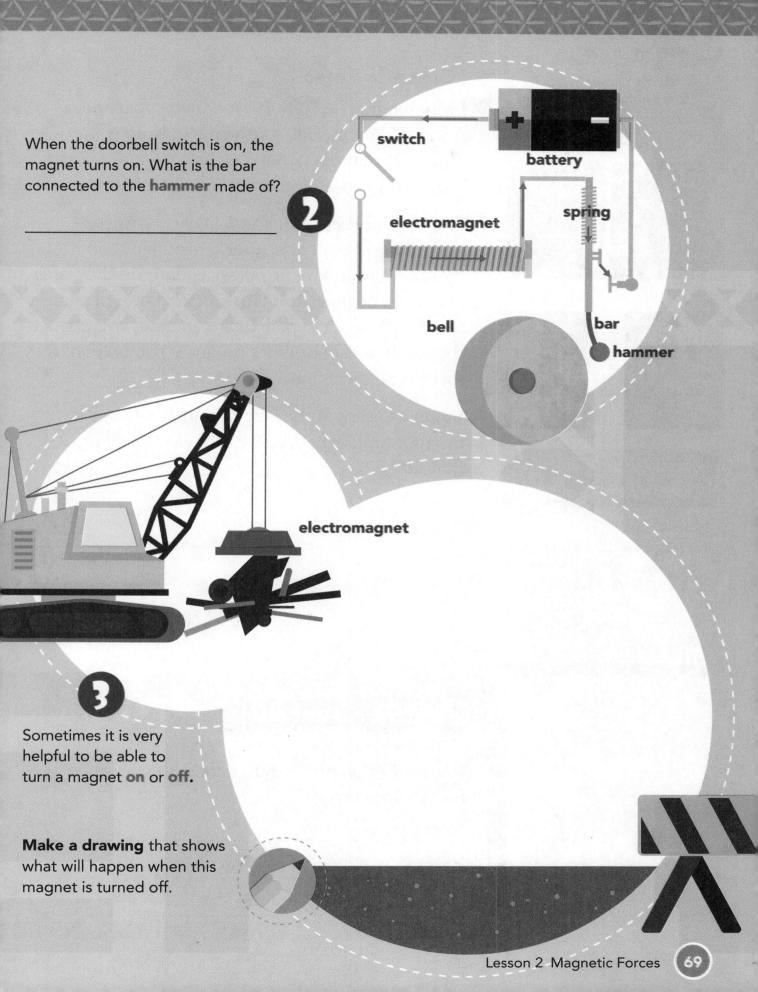

switch

battery

electromagnet

spring

bell

bar

hammer

electromagnet

3

Sometimes it is very helpful to be able to turn a magnet **on** or **off**.

Make a drawing that shows what will happen when this magnet is turned off.

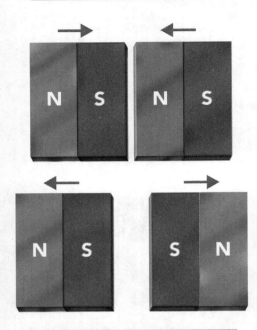

Crosscutting Concepts ▸ Toolbox

Cause and Effect
Compasses use magnetism to allow us to find our way around Earth. Identify the cause and effect relationship that makes a compass work.

Magnetic Poles

Every magnet has a north magnetic pole and a south magnetic pole. A **magnetic pole** is the point where the magnetic force is strongest. Earth is a large magnet with north and south poles.

Magnetic poles can interact. Objects **interact** when they affect each other. The interaction between two magnetic poles depends on the types of poles. The poles can either attract or repel one another. The north pole of one magnet will attract the south pole of another magnet. Two poles of the same type repel one another.

Compare How is the way that magnetic poles interact similar to the way that electric charges interact?

_____

_____

_____

Quest Connection

▼▼▼▼▼▼▼▼▼▼▼▼▼▼▼▼▼▼▼▼▼▼▼▼▼▼▼▼

How could the interaction of magnetic poles be used to lift a box?

_____

_____

_____

Magnetic Fields

A **magnetic field** is the space where the force of a magnet acts. The shape of the magnetic field depends on the shape of the magnet. You cannot see a magnetic field. But you can observe its effects. Hold a piece of iron close to a magnet. You will feel a pull. This pull is the magnetic force. Next, move the piece of metal a little closer to the magnet. The closer the metal gets to the magnet, the stronger the pull will be. The strength of a magnetic field changes with distance. It is strongest at the magnetic poles. The strength of the magnetic field gets stronger as the objects move closer.

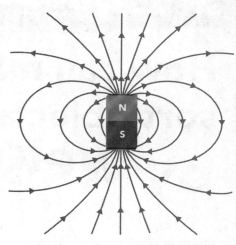

The lines show the magnetic field of the magnet. The lines are closer where the force is stronger.

✔️ Reading Check **Sequence** What happens if you move a magnet closer to a piece of metal?

_____

_____

✔️ Lesson 2 Check

1. **Explain** How can you use a magnet that has the north pole labeled to find the north pole of another magnet that has no marking?

_____

_____

_____

2. **Describe** What is one factor that affects the strength of magnetic forces between objects?

_____

_____

How can magnets sort objects by weight?

Your device will need to identify objects that have less weight than others. How does the weight of an object affect its interaction with a magnet?

Materials
- battery
- battery holder
- two pieces of copper wire
- iron nail
- switch
- balance, gram cubes, paper clips, staples, coins

Define the Problem

☐ 1. **SEP Define Problems** Define a problem that occurs when a magnet interacts with heavy objects.

_____

_____

☐ 2. **SEP Plan an Investigation** Make a plan to solve the problem. Use the materials. Include how you will test your object. Draw the design for your solution.

Engineering Practice

Engineers define problems to find solutions.

☐ **3.** Show your plan to your teacher before you begin. Build and test your device. Record your observations.

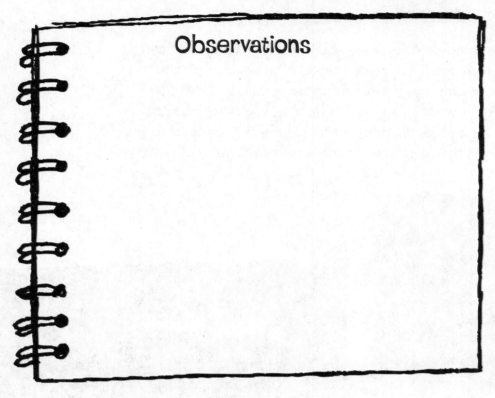

Observations

Evaluate Your Data

4. SEP Evaluate Your Design Did your solution solve the problem? Use evidence and reason to support your claim.

_____

_____

_____

5. Synthesize How could you use what you learned in this lab to use a magnet to sort boxes by weight?

_____

_____

_____

_____

uEngineer It! Build STEM

Moving Along

Phenomenon Some engineers design and build tools. These tools can be used in many places, including factories. They can be small tools that people carry with them. Or they can be much bigger. Steel factories use old metal objects to make new steel. At a steel factory, big machines sort the metal objects from other objects. Then machines move the metal to the right place. These machines that sort use magnets to move metal objects.

Build It

You work for a factory owner. You must make a tool to move steel objects from one place to another. The tool will pick up the steel objects and then drop them in a different place. The steel objects are mixed with other objects that are not made of steel. You will use a magnet in your device. Use the materials provided to build your tool.

☐ Make a drawing that shows the design of your tool. Write how you will test it. Show your drawing to your teacher before you start.

☐ Build and test your tool.

INTERACTIVITY

Complete an activity to support your Quest Findings.

STEM Weigh to Go

How can you use magnets to save time?

Design a Solution

Phenomenon Your device must separate heavy objects from lighter objects. It must use a force acting at a distance. Use what you learned in the Check-Ins to design the process that the factory can use to separate packages by weight. Write a step-by-step procedure to show how your solution works.

Communicate Your Solution

Decide how you will present your solution to the factory owner. Prepare your presentation. Explain how you used magnetic force to solve an engineering problem.

QUEST CHECK ✓ OFF

Systems Engineer

Systems engineers work on systems that have many parts or actions. A system can include machines, people, and computers. The parts of the system work together to do something that not only one machine or person can do.

Systems engineers figure out how to make the parts of the system work together. When the system is not working, they figure out why. The systems engineer has to understand all parts of the system. These include how machines work and how people use the machines. Many systems engineers are also computer engineers. This is because so many systems use computers.

📓 Write About It

In your science notebook, write an example of a system that affects your life. List some parts of the system.

1. **Predict** What will happen when a particle with a negative electric charge is placed near a particle with a positive electric charge?

    A. The particle with the positive charge will attract the particle with the negative charge.

    B. The particle with the positive charge will repel the particle with the negative charge.

    C. The positive charge on the particle will change into a negative charge.

    D. No change will happen.

2. **Explain** How can an object be neutral if it contains many particles that have a negative charge?

    _____

    _____

    _____

    _____

3. **Use Diagrams** This diagram shows what happens when a plastic rod with more negative charges is close to a metal plate.

    Which statement is true based on the diagram?

    A. The metal plate is an insulator.

    B. The metal plate is a conductor.

    C. The metal plate has gained negative charges.

    D. The metal plate has gained positive charges.

4. **Vocabulary** What happens during a static discharge?

    A. The electric force between objects gets stronger.

    B. Neutral objects gain a positive electric charge.

    C. Particles with an electric charge move between objects that are not touching.

    D. The number of charged particles in an object suddenly decreases.

5. Evaluate a Plan Your friend wants to use a magnet to hold the door of a playhouse closed. The door and the post beside the door are plastic. Will your friend's plan work? How can you make the plan better?

_____

_____

_____

_____

_____

_____

_____

_____

6. Use Evidence A student observes that a magnet is attracted to the door of a cabinet in the classroom. What conclusion can the student make from this observation?

   A. The cabinet is made of wood.

   B. The cabinet is positively charged.

   C. The cabinet is made of steel.

   D. The cabinet wall is a magnet.

The Essential Question *How can you solve a problem using magnetic forces?*

Show What You Learned

How do magnetic forces cause a compass to work?

_____

_____

_____

_____

_____

_____

_____

_____

_____

_____

A science group has 3 metal bars. One of the bars is a magnet with the north and south poles labeled with the letters N and S. The ends of the other bars were marked with the letters A and B on Bar 1 and the letters C and D on Bar 2.

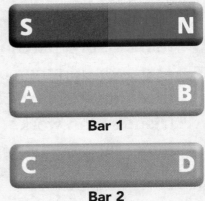

Bar 1

Bar 2

1. **Evaluate** The group investigated whether Bar 2 was a magnet. The only tool for the investigation was the magnet with labeled ends. One group member thought that they could decide by finding out whether Bar 2 and the magnet would stick together. Would this test provide enough data to decide whether Bar 2 is a magnet? Explain your answer.

   _____

   _____

   _____

2. **Define the Problem** How can the students use observations to decide whether a bar is a magnet?

   _____

   _____

   _____

3. **Cause and Effect** The north pole of the magnet and the Bar 1 end labeled A were placed next to each other. The two bars moved away from one another. What two conclusions could the students make about Bar 1?

   _____

   _____

The students then compared how the ends of Bar 2 interacted with the magnet. They brought different combinations of ends together. Their observations are shown in the table.

Interaction of magnet and Bar 2		
End of magnet	C	D
N	attract	attract
S	attract	attract

4. **Evaluate** What does the evidence on the table show about the end marked with the letter C?

   A. It is not part of a magnet.

   B. It is the north pole of a magnet.

   C. It is the south pole of a magnet.

   D. It could be a north or a south pole of a magnet.

5. **Cause and Effect** What conclusion can the group make based on the information in questions 3 and 4?

   A. Bar 1 is a magnet, and Bar 2 is not a magnet.

   B. Bar 2 is a magnet, and Bar 1 is not a magnet.

   C. Both bars are magnets.

   D. Both bars are not magnets.

How can you use a **force**?

Materials
- plastic ruler
- tape

Suggested Materials
- copper wire
- battery
- magnets
- iron nail
- paper clips
- staples

Phenomenon Scientists ask questions to investigate forces. How can you use a force to move an object 15 centimeters without touching it?

Plan Your Procedure

☐ **1.** Decide which force you want to use to move an object. Write a question about the force you want to investigate.

_____

_____

_____

Science Practice

Scientists ask questions that can be investigated.

☐ **2.** Write a procedure to answer your question. Show your procedure to your teacher before you begin.

_____

_____

_____

☐ **3.** Follow your procedure. Make changes in the procedure if it does not work the way you thought it would. Record your observations.

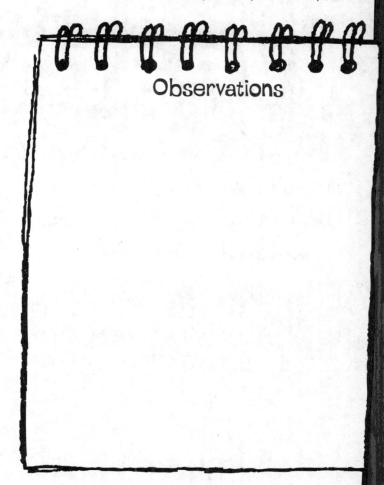
Evaluate Your Design

4. Describe What force did you use to move your object?

_____

_____

Observations

5. Analyze Explain why your procedure did or did not work.

_____

_____

_____

_____

_____

_____

_____

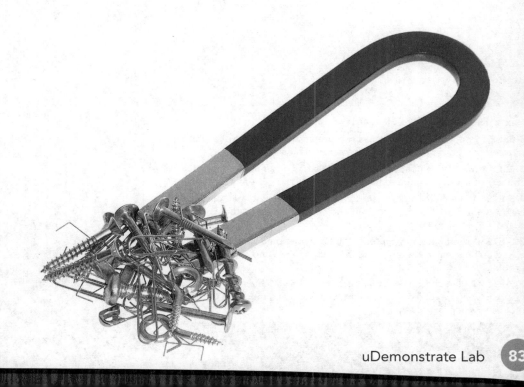

Weather

Next Generation Science Standards

3-ESS2-1 Represent data in tables and graphical displays to describe typical weather conditions expected during a particular season.

3-ESS3-1 Make a claim about the merit of a design solution that reduces the impacts of a weather-related hazard.

3-5-ETS1-1 Define a simple design problem reflecting a need or a want that includes specific criteria for success and constraints on materials, time, or cost.

3-5-ETS1-2 Generate and compare multiple possible solutions to a problem based on how well each is likely to meet the criteria and constraints of the problem.

3-5-ETS1-3 Plan and carry out fair tests in which variables are controlled and failure points are considered to identify aspects of a model or prototype that can be improved.

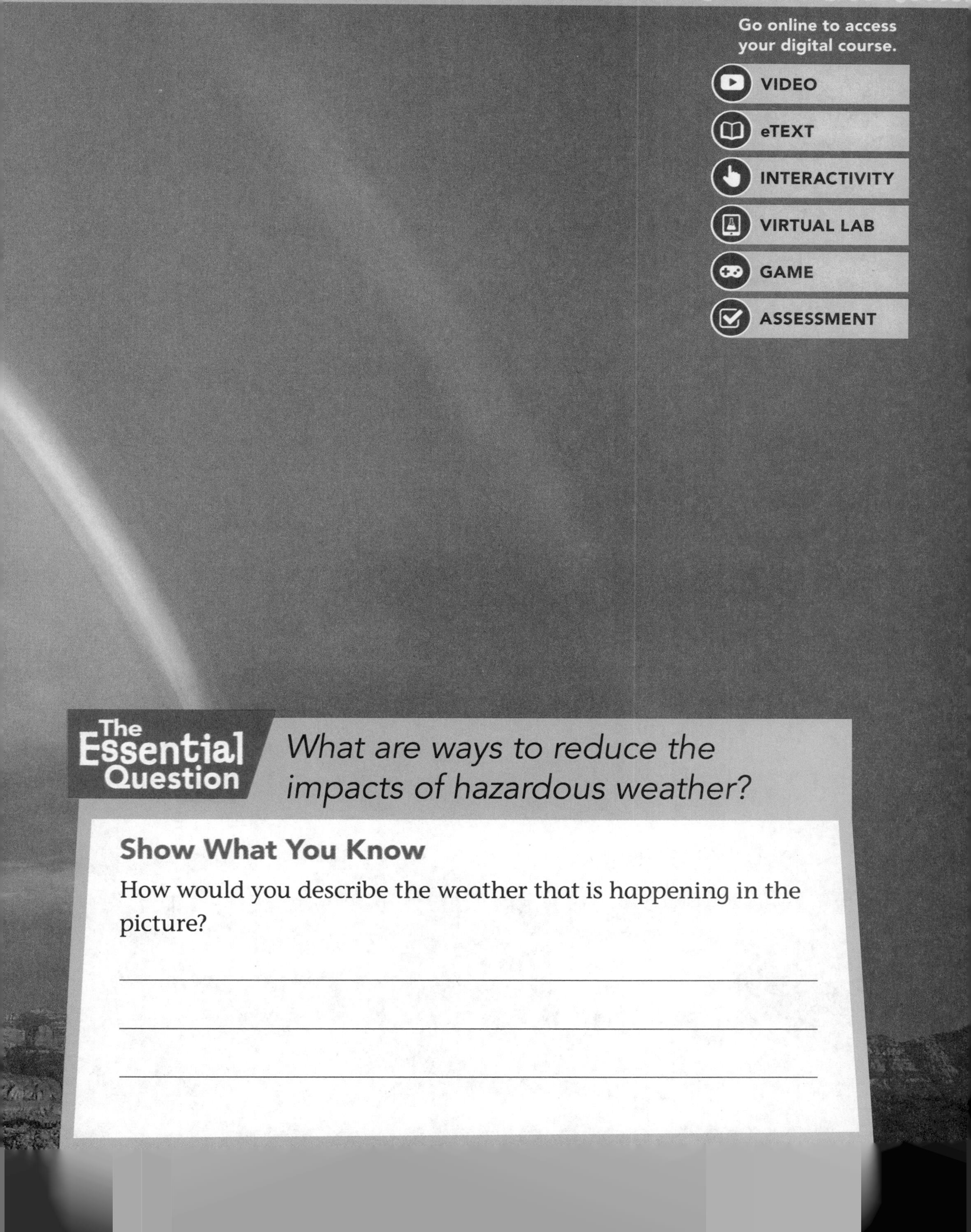

Go online to access your digital course.

▶ VIDEO

📖 eTEXT

👆 INTERACTIVITY

📱 VIRTUAL LAB

🎮 GAME

☑ ASSESSMENT

The Essential Question

What are ways to reduce the impacts of hazardous weather?

Show What You Know

How would you describe the weather that is happening in the picture?

_____

_____

_____

STEM

Hold on to Your Roof!

How can a roof best resist wind?

Phenomenon Hello, my name is Ezra Lin. I am an architect. My job is to design buildings. In this problem-solving learning activity, you will design a wind-resistant roof for a new house. To complete your Quest, you will decide which materials to use, present your design, and explain your solution.

Follow the path to learn how to complete the Quest. The Quest activities in the lessons will help you complete the Quest. Check off your progress on the path when you complete an activity with a QUEST CHECK ✓ OFF . Go online for more Quest activities.

Quest Check-In 1

Lesson 1
Explore how water can damage a roof.

Next Generation Science Standards
3-ESS3-1 Make a claim about the merit of a design solution that reduces the impacts of a weather-related hazard. (Also **3-5-ETS1-1**, **3-5-ETS1-2**, **3-5-ETS1-3**)

Quest Check-In Lab 3

Lesson 3

Choose materials and build models of different roofs. Test how well your models withstand strong winds.

Quest Check-In 2

Lesson 2

Find out how weather in different seasons can affect a roof. Find ways to protect a roof from different types of weather.

Quest Findings

Present your final design for a wind-resistant roof. Explain how your roof will protect the house from strong winds.

HANDS-ON LAB

3-ESS2-1, SEP.4

How can temperature damage a house?

Architects must know how temperature affects materials. How can water affect materials when it freezes?

Materials
- 100 mL plastic container with lid
- water
- crayon
- freezer

Procedure

☐ **1.** What do you think will happen to the amount of space water takes up if you freeze it? Write a prediction.

_____

_____

☐ **2.** Write a plan to use the materials to test your prediction. Show your plan to your teacher before you begin.

☐ **3.** Record your observations. Organize data from your plan in a table.

Analyze and Interpret Data

4. Apply What might happen to a home's water pipes if the water freezes? Cite data from the lab to support your answer.

_____

_____

_____

Science Practice

Scientists analyze and interpret data to identify relationships.

 Be careful with sharp edges.

Observations

Main Idea and Details

Literacy Connection

🎮 **GAME**

Practice what you learn with the Mini Games.

The most important information about a topic in a text is the main idea. Details tell more about the main idea. Here is how to identify the main idea and details in a text:

- Find the what or who that the text is about. This is the main idea.

- Look for sentences that describe more about the main idea. These are details that help you understand it.

Eyes in the Sky

Weather satellites help meteorologists predict weather. Weather satellites take photographs of Earth. They also collect data about the air. These data include how warm it is, how much moisture it has, and more. Weather scientists use the photographs and data to look for patterns. Computers help scientists analyze the data. Scientists and computers compare recent patterns to past weather patterns to predict future weather.

☑ **READING CHECK** **Main Idea and Details**
Circle the main idea of the text. Write one supporting detail you can find.

_____

_____

_____

Water and Weather

I can...

Explain how water affects weather.

3-ESS2-1

Literacy Skill
Main Idea and Details

Vocabulary
atmosphere
weather
humidity
evaporate
condense
precipitation

Academic Vocabulary
affect

 VIDEO

Watch a video about water and weather.

STEM Connection

The planet that you live on is different from any other place in our solar system. Earth is the only place in the solar system where water can naturally be found as a liquid, a solid, and a gas. These three states of water are key to Earth's weather.

Saturn's moon Titan also has weather, but it is very different from the weather on Earth! The main difference is that there is no water there. On Titan, you can still see clouds, rain, ice caps, lakes, and seas. But these are made of liquid methane, not water. Temperatures on Titan are much colder than here on Earth—about –179°C (–290°F). At that temperature, all water would be in the form of ice. Methane, however, does not freeze until it reaches –183°C (–295°F).

Write About It Suppose you had a space suit that allowed you to live on Titan. In your science notebook, tell what you think living there would be like.

Saturn's moon Titan

3-ESS2-1, SEP.4

How does the amount of water change over time?

Weather scientists must know how water changes as factors in the environment change. How can you investigate how fast water changes to a gas at room temperature?

Materials
- paper towel
- water
- balance
- gram cubes
- lab apron

Procedure

☐ **1.** Predict what will happen to the water in a wet paper towel over time.

_____

_____

⚠ Wear a lab apron.

Science Practice

Scientists analyze and interpret data to find answers.

☐ **2.** Plan how to use all the materials to test your prediction. Share your plan with your teacher before you begin. Record your observations in a table.

Analyze and Interpret Data

3. SEP Interpret Data Did the data from your experiment support your prediction? What do you think happened to the water?

_____

_____

_____

_____

_____

Observations

Water on Earth

From outer space, Earth looks mostly blue. That is because water covers about three-fourths of Earth's surface. Most of that water is in the ocean. Smaller amounts of water are in lakes, streams, and rivers. Water is also deep underground and in Earth's atmosphere. The **atmosphere** is the blanket of air that wraps around the planet. Water affects weather all over Earth. When you **affect** something, you change it. **Weather** is the condition of the atmosphere at a particular time and place.

Water in the atmosphere is most easily seen as clouds. But even when no clouds are in the sky, the atmosphere has water. The water in the atmosphere is a very small amount of all the water on Earth. This tiny amount, though, plays an important part in weather.

You can feel whether the air is dry or moist. How much water vapor is in the atmosphere is called **humidity**. A hot day can feel sticky if there is high humidity. Humidity and temperature in the atmosphere affect each other.

Define What is weather?

_____

_____

_____

_____

Literacy ▸ Toolbox

Main Idea and Details
The main idea of a text is the most important information. Underline the main idea of the paragraph.

Water Cycle

The movement of water on Earth is called the water cycle. A cycle is a group of events that happen in the same way over and over. Three main processes move water through the water cycle. Water from Earth's surface evaporates into the air. When water **evaporates**, it changes from a liquid to a gas called water vapor. Water in clouds **condenses**, or changes from a gas to a liquid. The liquid water leaving the clouds is called **precipitation**.

Identify Circle the process that moves water into the air.

Look at the diagram of the water cycle to find out how water moves and changes.

Water Cycle

Condensation
Water vapor particles join together and turn back into liquid form.

Precipitation
Water collects into drops. The drops become too heavy and fall back to Earth.

Evaporation
Water particles go into the air as water vapor. This process happens faster at higher temperatures.

How does precipitation form?

Rain, freezing rain, sleet, and snow form when water vapor interacts with different conditions in the air.

Write about each kind of precipitation.

Rain

....
....
....
....

Freezing rain

Freezing rain forms when rain makes contact with the ground that is 0°C (32°F).

warm air

cold air

Most clouds are made of ice crystals and water droplets.

Sleet

....
....
....
....

Snow

....
....
....
....

Quest Connection

Choose a type of precipitation. What affect might it have on a roof?

_____

_____

Weather

Water in the atmosphere affects weather. Bodies of water, such as oceans and lakes, also have an important effect on weather. Water can absorb heat and release heat into the atmosphere. Areas near water are warmer on cold days and cooler on hot days. These areas also tend to get more precipitation.

☑ **Reading Check** Main Idea and Details
What is the main idea of the paragraph?

_____

☑ Lesson 1 Check

1. **Summarize** How can water affect weather?

_____

_____

2. **Describe** What kinds of changes occur to water through the water cycle?

_____

_____

Rainy Weather **Is Coming**

It is important to consider weather's effects when building a house. Depending on where the house is built, rainy weather could be a problem. The roof you will design in this Quest must stand up to wind and rain. What kind of material should you use?

1. A roof can be made of straw, tin, tile, shingles, or many other materials. The table shows information about two different roof materials, and how well the materials perform when exposed to wind and water.

Weather Effect	Wood	Tin
Wind	is sturdy and heavy; will not blow away easily	can blow away in strong wind
Water	can absorb water	will not absorb water

2. Compare the materials. Which would be better for building a roof? Explain why you think one is a better solution.

_____

_____

_____

_____

μEngineer It! Define STEM

▶ **VIDEO**

Watch a video about some effects of hazardous weather.

Wild Weather!

Phenomenon Most days, the weather is not a problem. Winds in most areas are mild. Occasionally, though, weather can become extreme. Extreme winds can reach speeds much greater than normal. Winds can blow fast enough that they could blow across a football field in about one second! Extreme storms can have hazards other than strong winds. Rain, hail, and flooding often come with storms. When these storms happen, be ready! This means having a plan in case of an emergency. For architects, it means designing buildings to withstand extreme forces.

Define It

Suppose you are part of a town's weather safety group. The group is gathering information to make a weather safety website. Your task is to gather information about one kind of hazardous weather.

☐ Choose one type of hazardous weather to learn more about. Record your choice.

_____

☐ Research the hazards that the weather can cause.

_____

_____

☐ In the table, write what people might expect to happen in a weak storm, an average storm, and a strong storm.

Weak storm	
Average storm	
Strong storm	

☐ How can this information help engineers design buildings?

_____

_____

_____

Seasonal Weather Changes

I can...

Describe the weather conditions for each season.

3-ESS2-1

Literacy Skill
Main Idea and Details

Vocabulary
temperature
barometric pressure

Academic Vocabulary
predict

▶ **VIDEO**

Watch a video about seasonal weather changes.

STEM Connection

Would you like summer to last all year? If so, you have something in common with a long-distance champion! The Arctic tern is a bird that migrates farther than any other kind of bird. It travels from one end of Earth to the other, and back again, every year.

Each April or May, Arctic terns arrive in the Arctic. It is summer there. The sun shines all day and night. The terns lay their eggs in nests on the ground. Their chicks hatch in about three weeks. The parents can be seen diving headfirst into frigid waters to catch fish for the young. In just a few weeks as cooler weather is near, the young terns will travel all the way to Antarctica where summer is just beginning. That is a 20,000-kilometer (12,400-mile) trip! When summer at Antarctica ends, the terns fly all the way back for the Arctic summer.

Explain Why do Arctic terns make the long trip twice each year?

_____

_____

_____

When is the air dry?

Scientists identify patterns to help them understand how things work. What pattern can you find between air temperature and the amount of water in the air?

Materials
• computer with Internet connection
• graph paper
• City Weather sheet

Procedure

☐ **1.** Choose a city that you would like to study. Write the city's name at the top of the table on the City Weather sheet.

☐ **2.** **SEP Obtain Information** With the help of an adult, use the Internet to find the temperature and humidity for your city on the first day of each month for the last year. Record the information on the City Weather sheet.

☐ **3.** On the graph paper, make two bar graphs. On one graph, record the month and temperature. On the other graph, record the month and the humidity.

Science Practice

Scientists analyze and interpret data to identify patterns.

Analyze and Interpret Data

4. CCC Patterns Describe any pattern you see in your data.

_____

_____

_____

_____

_____

Weather and Seasons

Weather is an important part of everyone's life. It affects what we wear, what we do, and where and how we live. We cannot control weather, but we can predict it. When you **predict** something, you tell what is likely going to happen in the future. Predicting the weather helps us be prepared for whatever comes our way.

One way to predict weather is to know what kind of weather most likely happens each season of the year. Earth's year is divided into four seasons—summer, fall, winter, and spring. In some places, such as Hawaii, weather changes little from one season to the next. In most of the United States, weather is different during each season. Temperatures in winter can be 40°C (104°F) colder than temperatures in summer. **Temperature** is a measure of how hot or cold something is.

📖 **Reflect** In your science notebook, tell how today's weather affected you.

Quest Connection

An architect from a different part of the country is building a home in your area. What should the architect know about the weather there?

_____

_____

_____

Weather Graphs

Weather scientists have to communicate their findings. Sometimes, the best way to do that is with graphs. Graphs can show the weather over a few days, or even longer. Graphs that show a whole year are good at showing seasonal weather changes.

Use Graphs Make a bar graph using the data in the table about average precipitation in London, England. Your graph will describe average precipitation during different months and seasons.

	Jan	Feb	Mar	Apr	May	Jun	Jul	Aug	Sep	Oct	Nov	Dec
Average precipitation in cm	10	7	9	8	8	8	6	6	8	9	9	10

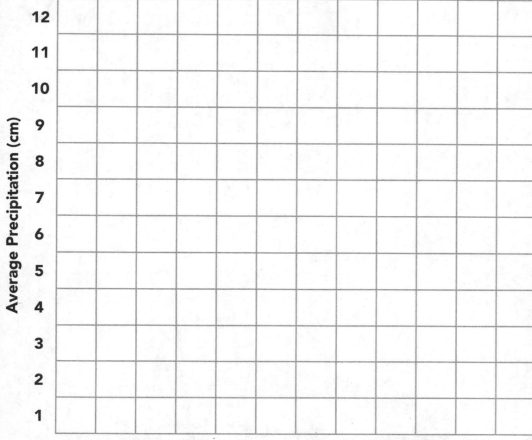

How can a snowstorm affect you?

Snow, ice, and freezing rain become more common during winter. When weather changes, it can have an impact on your daily life. How can you prepare for a snowstorm?

Match each numbered solution to the snowstorm problem it solves.

_____ slippery, icy sidewalks

_____ doors and windows let in cold air

_____ cold inside the house

_____ cannot look up temperature on the Internet because it is down

Simple Weather Instruments

To predict weather, scientists gather information about the current weather conditions. They gather information about factors that affect weather, such as temperature, humidity, and barometric pressure. **Barometric pressure** is the weight of the air pushing down on anything beneath it. Air is pushing down on you right now, but you cannot feel it. Barometric pressure is measured with a barometer. A higher number on the barometer means a greater push by the air.

Scientists look for patterns in the weather data they collect. They compare those patterns to weather patterns from the past. Comparing patterns helps them identify what the weather will most likely be.

✓ Reading Check **Main Idea and Details** What are three weather factors that scientists measure?

_____

_____

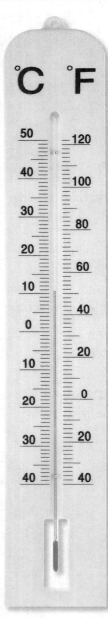

Temperature can be measured in degrees Celsius (°C) or degrees Fahrenheit (°F). The temperature on this thermometer is_____°C or _____°F.

A barometer measures the weight of air pushing down on objects.

A hygrometer measures humidity.

Weather Satellites

Not all weather instruments are simple. Weather satellites like this one hover over Earth. They can gather information over very large parts of Earth's surface. The information includes cloud patterns, air movement, ground and sea temperatures, and other factors. The information they gather can be data or pictures, like this one showing a hurricane from space.

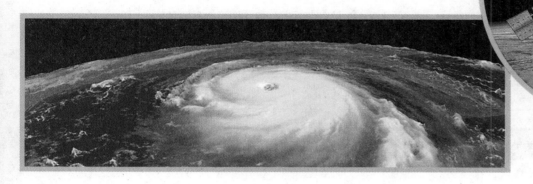

☑ Lesson 2 Check

1. **Describe** How is weather during the year in most of the United States different from the weather in Hawaii?

2. **Explain** Suppose you are going to visit another state in the fall. How can you use a weather graph to predict what the weather will be like when you visit?

A Roof for All Seasons

People and animals can move away from bad weather, but buildings cannot. Once a home is built, it has to withstand any weather that comes its way. The roof of a house may be damaged by high temperatures in summer, rain and wind in spring and fall, and large amounts of snow in winter. Record the material you chose for a roof in Check-In 1. In the table, list how weather in different seasons might affect the material and damage the roof. Come up with a way to protect the material for each problem.

Material for roof _____

Season	How weather may affect the roof	How to protect the roof
Summer		
Fall		
Winter		
Spring		

QUEST CHECK ✔ OFF

Weather Whiplash

There is an expression used about the weather in many places: "If you do not like the weather, wait 15 minutes." It is true that weather is always changing and can change quickly. People in the Midwest region of the United States know this very well.

In 1911, Oklahoma City set two record temperatures in one day! On November 11, 1911, the temperature was 28°C (83°F) in the afternoon. That was the highest temperature ever for that day of the year. Later that day, cold air moved into the area. The temperature dropped all the way to −8°C (17°F). That was the coldest temperature ever recorded for that date! The weather went from summer-like temperatures to below freezing in a matter of hours. Similar temperature changes were felt all around the region. This event is known today as the Great Blue Norther of 1911.

Predict What might happen to a home if a weather event like the Great Blue Norther occurred?

_____

_____

_____

Weather Hazards

STEM Connection

Flash! Boom! A severe thunderstorm has hit your area. Communications systems might stop working. Roads and buildings might be damaged or destroyed. Hazardous weather conditions that cause major damage are sometimes called disasters. When a disaster occurs, the government steps in to help. The Federal Emergency Management Agency, or FEMA, serves people affected by disasters. FEMA might put up shelters, bring in food and water, help people find family members, provide access to medical help, or even more. It is important to have a lot of help in a disaster. The effects of a disaster are bigger than a person alone can fix.

Identify Who are some people in your community that might help during a major weather disaster?

_____

_____

STEM · uInvestigate Lab

How can you stop a flood?

Engineers test the properties of different materials to decide which are best for certain jobs. How can you find out which materials would be best for flood control?

Plan Your Procedure

☐ **1.** Which materials can you use to control flooding? Brainstorm ways to test three of the suggested materials to see which one is the best solution.

☐ **2.** Write a plan to test the materials. Make sure you control variables so that the tests are fair. Have your teacher approve your plan before you begin.

☐ **3.** Use your plan to test the materials. Record your observations in a table on a separate sheet of paper.

Evaluate Your Solution

4. SEP Evaluate Compare results with your classmates. Which materials were the most effective at stopping water? What properties did the effective materials share?

_____

_____

5. How could you improve the most effective materials?

_____

_____

Materials
- plastic tray
- ruler
- water
- masking tape

Suggested Materials
- jar
- wire mesh
- cloth
- plastic sheet
- sandpaper
- tile

Engineering Practice

Engineers identify and control variables when they investigate.

Storms

Look at clouds and you might notice they do not stay in one place very long. The atmosphere is constantly in motion. Energy from the sun and differences in air pressure cause air to move. With a lot of energy in the atmosphere and big differences in air pressure, winds can blow very fast. Sometimes, a storm can occur. A **storm** is a disturbance in the atmosphere with a lot of wind. Storms usually carry a large amount of precipitation as well. Heavy rains can cause **floods**. This means that water in certain places is too high and may be causing damage. Major storms can have a big **impact**, or effect, on an area. People design different solutions to reduce impacts.

One of the strongest and largest types of storms is a **hurricane**. Hurricanes form over warm ocean water and have very strong winds. It is important to be prepared if a hurricane comes close to your home.

☑ **Reading Check** **Main Idea and Details**
Underline two details that tell why a storm can have a big impact.

Quest Connection

What are some ways that a roof can keep you safe in a storm?

_____

_____

Reduce the Impact

A hurricane is coming! Hurricanes can be very dangerous. The winds can move houses, cars, boats, trees, and other objects—including people. How can you be prepared for a hurricane?

A lightning rod attracts lightning to keep buildings safe.

Boards protect the windows from objects blown by the storm.

Flood walls made of sandbags, or other materials can keep water away from homes.

Seawalls can prevent floods from ocean waters.

Plan It! You are building a house in an area that has hurricanes. Plan your house! List some criteria for your house.

_____

_____

_____

_____

_____

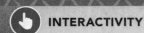
Thunderstorms and Tornadoes

Thunderstorms are extreme storms that happen in many parts of the world. These storms have thunder and lightning. Have you have ever gotten a shock when you touched metal after walking over a carpet? If so, you have experienced the same process that causes lightning. But lightning is much stronger! Lightning happens when the electricity moves from a cloud. As the electricity moves toward the ground, it causes light and heat. The heat from lightning causes air particles to move apart very fast. That is when you hear the BOOM of thunder. Thunderstorms often come with heavy rains. They can also cause large pieces of ice, called hailstones, to fall as precipitation.

Another hazardous storm that can happen with a thunderstorm is a **tornado**—a large mass of swirling wind such as the one in the photo. Tornadoes form over land when large amounts of warm and cold air mix. Tornadoes can have the fastest winds on Earth. They swirl in a funnel that reaches from the clouds to the ground.

Explain Why are tornadoes and thunderstorms dangerous?

_____

_____

_____

Drought

The storm in the photo is not carrying rain. It is blowing a huge cloud of dust! Sandstorms and dust storms occur in very dry environments. Violent winds lift large amounts of sand or dust into the atmosphere. The storm can happen if a **drought**, or a long period with little to no rain, occurs.

A huge dust storm occurred in the United States on April 14, 1935. The storm turned daylight into a sky dark as night. In some places, the darkness was so black that people could not see their own hands! The storm traveled hundreds of miles. That day in history is now known as Black Sunday.

Write About It How can you stay safe in a storm? In your science notebook, make a plan for how you can be ready if a major storm hits your area.

☑ Lesson 3 Check

1. **Describe** What are two ways to stay safe during hazardous weather?

_____

_____

_____

2. **Identify** How can people reduce the impact of a flood?

_____

_____

_____

How can a roof be improved?

This next step in your Quest is to make two designs for a wind-resistant roof. You will build your model roofs and test them. You will use evidence from your tests to decide which design is the best.

Materials
- fan
- cardboard box
- safety goggles

Suggested Materials
- craft sticks
- glue
- cardboard
- plastic
- construction paper
- stopwatch

Build Your Model

☐ **1.** What do you think the most important criteria will be in designing your roofs?

_____

_____

_____

☐ **2. SEP Design Solutions** Think about your criteria. Select the materials you will use to build your roofs. Draw a plan for each roof.

Engineering Practice

Engineers build models to test solutions.

⚠ Be careful using the fan.

⚠ Wear safety goggles.

☐ 3. **SEP Develop and Use Models** Build your roof models. Then take them to the model house to test them. Record your observations.

Evaluate Your Model

4. **SEP Construct an Explanation** Use your test results to compare solutions with your classmates. What kinds of roof materials and designs resisted strong winds the best?

_____

_____

_____

_____

5. **SEP Evaluate Information** What could you do to improve your design?

_____

_____

_____

INTERACTIVITY

Find out how to hold on to a roof.

STEM ▶ # Hold on to **your roof!**

How can a roof best resist wind?

Phenomenon It is time to present your final design for a wind-resistant roof. Use what you learned in this topic. Use evidence from your tests to decide on the best design.

☐ Draw a plan for your design. Be sure to include all necessary details.

☐ Present your design to your classmates. Explain how your design solution will reduce the impact of heavy winds on a roof. Make sure your explanation is based on evidence you gathered.

QUEST CHECK ✓ OFF

Architect

Architects are professionals who design homes and buildings. Sometimes they design large buildings, such as skyscrapers. Other times they design private homes or other smaller buildings. Their designs are called blueprints and show every detail about the structure they are building. The measurements on the blueprints are followed by the builder exactly as drawn.

Architects are detail-oriented people. Much of an architect's work involves science. Architects must know how to support a lot of weight. They need to know which materials can support their buildings. Architects go to special schools to learn what they need to know. Some architects, like Frank Lloyd Wright and I. M. Pei, are famous for their unique designs. If you want to see your ideas built in real life, you might like to be an architect.

📓 In your science notebook, write whether you would like to be an architect. Explain your answer.

☑ Assessment

1. **Vocabulary** When liquid water turns into water vapor, what is the process called?

   A. evaporation

   B. condensation

   C. precipitation

   D. water cycle

2. **Explain** What are two different ways that water affects weather?

   _____

   _____

   _____

   _____

3. **Describe** What are two differences that happen when fall changes to winter?

   _____

   _____

   _____

   _____

4. **Identify** Which statement describes a way to stay safe in hazardous weather?

   A. Wait until you see lightning to go indoors.

   B. Install a lightning rod on a roof before a storm comes.

   C. Open windows in your house during high winds.

   D. Cover windows with boards when it rains.

5. **Apply Concepts** Edmund wants to know what kind of weather to expect in New York City when he goes there. He is planning to visit in three months. Which of these choices describes the **best** source of information for Edmund to use?

   A. a forecast in the newspaper

   B. satellite photos of cloud patterns

   C. a map showing recent weather systems

   D. a weather chart showing seasonal weather

Use the table to answer questions 6 and 7.

Forecast

Thursday	Friday	Saturday	Sunday
☀	⛅	⛅	🌧
4°C (39°F) 1°C (34°F)	6°C (43°F) -2°C (28°F)	10°C (50°F) 3°C (37°F)	15°C (59°F) 4°C (39°F)

6. Describe What will the weather be like on Saturday and Sunday?

_____

_____

_____

_____

_____

_____

_____

7. Interpret Which day is likely to have the highest humidity?

   A. Thursday

   B. Friday

   C. Saturday

   D. Sunday

What are ways to reduce the impacts of hazardous weather?

Show What You Learned

Thunderstorms can sometimes drop hazardous amounts of rain. What would one impact from such a storm be? How could people reduce the impact of the storm?

_____

_____

_____

_____

_____

_____

_____

_____

_____

_____

_____

The tables show weather data for three different cities. Use the data in the tables to answer questions 1–4.

City 1			
	Average high temperature (°C/°F)	Average low temperature (°C/°F)	Average seasonal precipitation (cm)
January–March	2/36	−6/21	5
April–June	18/64	8/46	6
July–September	25/77	16/61	9
October–December	8/46	7/45	6

City 2			
	Average high temperature (°C/°F)	Average low temperature (°C/°F)	Average seasonal precipitation (cm)
January–March	18/64	5/41	9
April–June	28/82	17/63	10
July–September	31/88	22/72	17
October–December	21/70	9/48	8

City 3			
	Average high temperature (°C/°F)	Average low temperature (°C/°F)	Average seasonal precipitation (cm)
January–March	2/36	−6/21	5
April–June	18/64		9
July–September	25/77	17/63	8
October–December	9/48	1/34	6

1. **Patterns** Your friend is planning a trip to City 2 for next July. What kind of weather should your friend prepare for?

    A. hot, dry weather

    B. hot, wet weather

    C. cool, dry weather

    D. cool, wet weather

2. **Patterns** Two of the cities listed are in the same region of the country. Which two cities are in a similar region?

    _____

    _____

3. **Use Evidence** What evidence supports your answer to question 3?

    _____

    _____

    _____

4. **Patterns** The average low temperature for April to June in City 3 is missing. Which choice is most likely the missing data?

    A. 18/64

    B. 21/70

    C. 10/50

    D. 2/36

uDemonstrate Lab

What can barometric pressure tell you?

Materials
- jar
- balloon
- scissors
- tape
- plastic stirrer
- index card

Phenomenon Scientists design and use tools to gather data. How can you build and use a tool to measure the weather?

Procedure

Science Practice

Scientists analyze and interpret data to identify relationships.

☐ **1. SEP Design Solutions** How can you use the materials to build a barometer? Describe or draw your design and have your teacher approve it.

 Be careful using scissors.

☐ **2.** Build your barometer.

☐ **3.** Make a plan to use the barometer to observe and measure changes in the weather. Write your plan and have your teacher approve it.

_____

_____

_____

_____

☐ **4.** Conduct your investigation. Record your observations in a table.

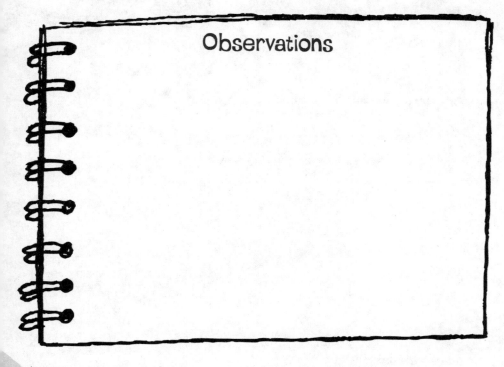

Observations

Analyze and Interpret Data

5. CCC Patterns Look at your observations. What pattern can you identify between your measurements and the weather?

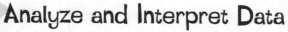

_____

_____

_____

6. CCC Patterns Based on the pattern you observe, how could you use your barometer to avoid bad weather?

_____

_____

_____

Climate

Next Generation Science Standards

3-ESS2-2 Obtain and combine information to describe climates in different regions of the world.

Go online to access
your digital course.

▶ VIDEO

📖 eTEXT

👆 INTERACTIVITY

📱 VIRTUAL LAB

🎮 GAME

☑ ASSESSMENT

The Essential Question

How can you explain what climate is like in different places?

Show What You Know

How can you describe what the weather is like where polar bears live?

_____

_____

_____

Climates on Location

Where should we film a movie?

Phenomenon Hello there! My name is James Scotto. I am a movie location scout. I travel around the world to find amazing places to film different movies. I need your help to choose locations for a new movie. The movie will take place throughout a whole year. It needs to feature different weather. It also needs to be filmed in just a few months.

In this Quest, you will identify what the actors can do in different kinds of weather. You will use patterns to select locations for filming.

Follow the path to learn how to complete the Quest. The Quest activities in the lessons will help you complete the Quest. Check off your progress on the path when you complete an activity with a QUEST CHECK ✔ OFF . Go online for more Quest activities.

Quest Check-In 1

Lesson 1

Think about some different scenes the movie will need. Identify the types of weather that should be featured in the movie.

Next Generation Science Standards
3-ESS2-2 Obtain and combine information to describe climates in different regions of the world.

VIDEO

Watch a video about a movie location scout.

Quest Check-In 3

Lesson 3

Compare the climates of different possible filming locations.

Quest Check-In Lab 2

Lesson 2

Examine how and why glaciers change. Suggest how you could use this change in the movie.

Quest Findings

Present your research! Tell the movie producer where you want to film. Explain why you chose the locations.

How does temperature change on a mountain?

Scientists look for patterns in data to help explain why things happen. How do patterns explain differences in temperature on a mountain?

Materials
- Elevation and Temperature Map sheet

Procedure

☐ **1.** What kind of information do the maps show?

_____

☐ **2.** Use the maps to see if there is a pattern between how high something is and temperature. Collect data in the table.

Science Practice

Scientists combine information from multiple sources to explain natural phenomena.

Analyze and Interpret Data

3. CCC Patterns What pattern do you see? Did your classmates find the same pattern?

_____

_____

Compare and Contrast

When you compare and contrast, you identify how things are alike and different. When you compare, you find how they are alike. When you contrast, you find how they are different.

Read the paragraph about weather and climate.

caribou

🎮 **GAME**

Practice what you learn with the Mini Games.

Weather and Climate

Weather is always happening. It is always changing too. One moment you may be sitting on a beach. The weather is warm and sunny. Suddenly winds begin to blow. Rain clouds cover the sky. The weather quickly becomes cold and rainy. It is time to leave the beach!

You can come back the next day because you know the beach is usually sunny and warm. Climate is what kind of weather a place usually has over a long time. Every location has a climate. Some places get very cold. Other places are very warm. This caribou has thick fur because its home is usually very cold. Climates are always changing too, but it takes a longer time to happen. Climates change much more slowly than weather.

☑ **READING CHECK** **Compare and Contrast**
Underline information that you could use to compare weather and climate. Circle information that could help you contrast them.

Climates

Describe some factors that affect climate.
3-ESS2-2

Literacy Skill
Compare and Contrast

Vocabulary
climate
polar
temperate
tropical
equator
latitude
elevation

▶ **VIDEO**
Watch a video about climate.

SPORTS ▶ Connection

How far would you have to go to find a different climate? If you are climbing a mountain, you might not have to go far. According to one climate classification system, Earth has 14 different kinds of climate. Ten of them are on the Big Island of Hawaii!

The east shore of the island is warm and wet all year. As you move west on the island, the road quickly climbs higher. The weather gets drier and cooler as you walk. You are actually hiking up Mauna Kea volcano. The visitor center is 2,800 meters above sea level. The few plants there are very different from those at lower levels. If you hike to the top of Mauna Kea, you will be more than 4,200 meters above sea level. The weather there is always cold and very dry. Walk west and down the mountain. You will find a hot desert.

Infer What is one reason that the Big Island of Hawaii has so many different climate zones?

_____

_____

How does the sun's radiation vary on Earth's surface?

Materials
- flashlight
- ball
- colored tape

Scientists use models to collect evidence and draw conclusions. How does Earth's tilt affect the amount of sunlight different places get?

Science Practice

Scientists *communicate information* to explain the evidence.

Procedure

☐ **1.** Write a prediction about how Earth's tilt on its axis affects the amount of sunlight different parts of Earth get.

_____

_____

☐ **2. SEP Plan an Investigation** Make a plan to use the materials to test your prediction. Show your plan to your teacher before you begin. Record your observations.

Observations

Analyze and Interpret Data

3. SEP Communicate Turn to another student and explain how Earth's tilt affects the amount of sunlight it gets. Use evidence from your model in your explanation.

Climate Characteristics

Can you predict what the weather will be next month or next season? There is no way to know exactly. You might be able to make a good guess, though. We know what weather will most likely be like at a certain time and place during each part of the year. Scientists have gathered data that show that weather follows certain patterns. The pattern of weather conditions that occur in a certain area over a long period is called **climate**. A climate is usually described as average temperature and precipitation.

Not all of Earth has the same climate. Each region of Earth has its own type of climate. Earth's main climate regions are polar, temperate, and tropical. A **polar** climate is very cold and dry. A **temperate** climate is mild. It usually has big differences between seasonal weather patterns. A **tropical** climate is warm throughout the year. A main factor that determines whether climate is polar, temperate, or tropical is where on Earth the place is located.

☑ **READING CHECK** **Compare and Contrast** What are the two main differences in the three climate regions? How are they similar?

_____

_____

_____

_____

The Sun and Climate

The sun constantly sends energy toward Earth. This energy heats Earth's atmosphere, water, and land. Each of these Earth systems heats differently. The differences in heating patterns affect weather and climate.

Not every place on Earth gets an equal share of the sun's energy. Areas closest to the equator get the most energy. The **equator** is an imaginary line around the middle of the planet. It divides Earth into northern and southern halves. The areas farthest from the equator, the North Pole and the South Pole, get the least amount of the sun's energy. These patterns cause climates to be more extreme near the equator and Earth's Poles.

Identify How does the sun affect climate?

_____

_____

_____

Crosscutting Concepts ▸ Toolbox

Patterns Scientists look for patterns in nature to understand why things happen. Compare the climate where you live with the climate of a different place. How are the patterns alike? How are they different?

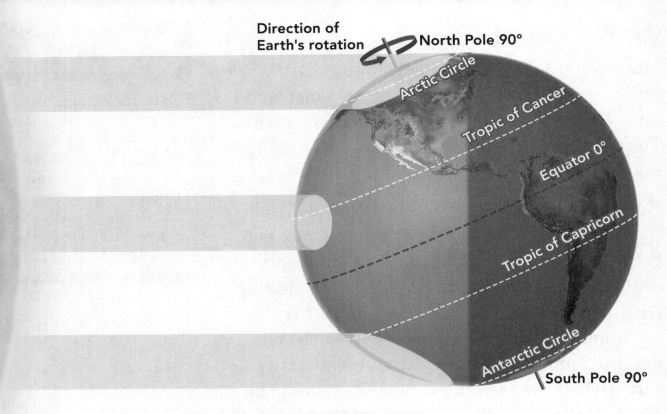

Direction of Earth's rotation

North Pole 90°

Arctic Circle

Tropic of Cancer

Equator 0°

Tropic of Capricorn

Antarctic Circle

South Pole 90°

Latitude and Climate

Latitude is a measure of how far north or south of the equator a place is. Latitude is written in degrees north or south. Key West, Florida, for example, is about 24 degrees north of the equator, or 24° N. A location's latitude has a big effect on its climate.

In the diagram, the North Pole is tilted toward the sun. It is the start of summer in the Northern Hemisphere, around June 21. The area north of the Arctic Circle will get sunlight all day long. At the start of winter, around December 21, this area will receive no direct sunlight at all. At the start of summer in the Arctic, it will be dark all day long in the area south of the Antarctic Circle. Seasons north and south of the equator are opposite.

Infer The latitude of the Arctic Circle is 66° N. What is the latitude of the Antarctic Circle?

The Ocean and Climate

About 70 percent of Earth is covered by ocean water. The sun's energy warms the ocean water. As the water warms, it evaporates more quickly into the atmosphere. Winds then move the water over land. Eventually, the water falls as precipitation. This is why areas near the ocean usually get more precipitation.

Lands near the ocean have milder winters and cooler summers than lands in the middle of continents. This is because water changes temperature more slowly than land. In the winter, the ocean is warmer than the land. In the summer, the ocean is cooler than the land.

Cause and Effect How does the ocean affect climate?

_____

_____

......**uBe a Scientist**............

Evaporation Investigation
With an adult, put the same amount of water in two bowls. Use a fan or a light source on one bowl. What do you observe about the rate of evaporation? What can you infer about climate from your results?

Quest Connection

▼▼▼▼▼▼▼▼▼▼▼▼▼▼▼▼▼▼▼▼▼▼▼▼▼▼▼

If you were to film a movie near the ocean, what kinds of weather should you expect?

_____

_____

_____

_____

Land Features and Climate

Mountaineers—people who climb mountains—must be prepared for constant changes in temperature as they climb. Higher elevations tend to be colder. **Elevation** is the measure of how high above ground something is. At sea level, elevation is zero. As the mountaineers climb up the mountain, temperatures get colder. The temperature at the bottom of a mountain might be 0 °C (32 °F). At the top of the same mountain, the temperature might be –15 °C (5 °F).

Tall mountains affect climate in another way. Winds generally flow in the same direction. As wind moves toward a mountain, the air slows and moves upward and over the mountain. The side of the mountain that the wind reaches first will get plenty of rain. The other side will get little rain. The reason is because the air cools as it moves upward. Precipitation forms in the cooler air.

Draw Conclusions Suppose wind moves toward a mountain from west to east. Would the east or west side of the mountain get more rain? Why?

_____

_____

_____

_____

_____

Draw and Analyze Graphs

The climate of one place on Earth can be very different from the climate of another place. The table has information about the temperature and the amount of precipitation in two different cities in summer and in winter.

City	Average summer temperature	Average winter temperature	Average summer precipitation	Average winter precipitation
New York	28°C (82°F)	5°C (41°F)	10 cm	9 cm
San Francisco	20°C (68°F)	15°C (59°F)	1 cm	11 cm

1. Draw two bar graphs that compare the temperatures in New York and San Francisco.

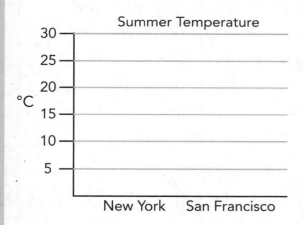

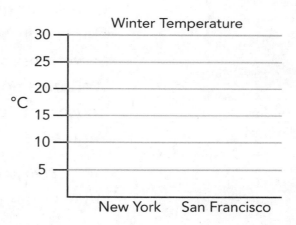

2. Draw two bar graphs that compare precipitation in New York and San Francisco.

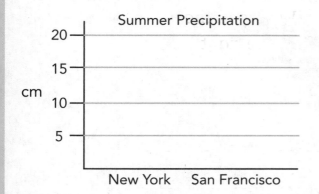

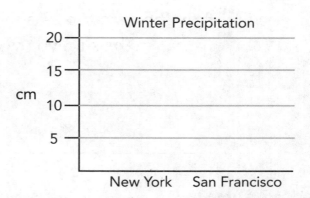

Climate Change

I can...

Describe ways in which climates can change.
Explain how the global climate is changing.

3-ESS2-2

Literacy Skill
Compare and Contrast

Vocabulary
greenhouse effect
greenhouse gas
climate change

VIDEO

Watch a video about climate change.

STEM Connection

Scientific data indicate that the climate of Earth is getting warmer. This change has caused several changes in the Earth system. For example, the level of water in the ocean is rising. Higher ocean levels can cause flooding in cities and towns near the seashore. Usually, the floods happen during a storm.

Wetlands—a type of ecosystem—help prevent floods. Wetlands are areas that are covered with water at least part of the year. Wetland plants filter water. Many kinds of animals live in wetlands for some or all of their life cycle. Wetlands have been destroyed as people build houses and other structures. Scientists and engineers work to build new wetlands.

Infer Many wetland plants have deep roots. How do the roots protect the soil?

_____

_____

uInvestigate Lab

What do tree rings show?

Scientists collect data, draw conclusions, and then share their findings. How can you use data to determine the age of a tree?

Materials
- Weather Data sheet

Suggested Materials
- colored pencils
- ruler

Procedure

☐ 1. **CCC Scale, Proportion, and Quantity** A tree trunk makes a ring each year that it grows. About how old is this tree? _____

☐ 2. **CCC Cause and Effect** Predict how temperature and precipitation affect tree growth.

_____

_____

Science Practice

Scientists gather information from different sources.

☐ 3. Use the Weather Data sheet and other materials to gather information to test your prediction.

Analyze and Interpret Data

4. **Discuss** How can you use tree rings to learn about the climate of an area?

_____

_____

5. **SEP Explain** How could scientists use tree rings to study changes in an area?

_____

_____

_____

What is the greenhouse effect?

In a garden greenhouse, a glass ceiling and walls allow some energy from sunlight to be trapped and warm the inside of the building. The **greenhouse effect** describes how the atmosphere traps energy from sunlight and keeps Earth warm, similar to a garden greenhouse.

Certain gases in the atmosphere, called **greenhouse gases**, help trap some of the energy in the atmosphere. Some energy not trapped by greenhouse gases is absorbed by the ground or water on Earth. All of the energy on Earth that came from the sun eventually goes back into space.

atmosphere

Draw the paths of energy from the sun to the greenhouse to demonstrate how the greenhouse effect works.

greenhouse gases

Climate Change Investigation Use a thermometer to measure the air temperature in a sunny place. Then use a folder to block sunlight and measure the temperature again. How could volcano ash blocking sunlight affect climate?

Natural Factors and Climate Change

Scientists have gathered data about the climate of Earth over time. The data support the idea that Earth's temperature has changed during Earth's history. Over a long time, a place can become hotter or colder. The amount of precipitation can also change. **Climate change** is a change in temperature, precipitation, or other weather patterns over a long time. Some climate changes happen because of natural causes. Volcanoes can release ash and other particles that block sunlight. Then the surface of Earth can become cooler.

Write About It In your science notebook, tell other ways natural factors could cause climate change.

Quest Connection

How could you show the causes of climate change in your movie?

_____

_____

_____

Humans and Climate Change

Human activities can also change climate. When we burn fuels for heat, transportation, or electricity, carbon dioxide is produced. Carbon dioxide is a greenhouse gas. Greenhouse gases trap heat in Earth's atmosphere. Some heat in the atmosphere is good. It is why life can exist on Earth. But scientists have evidence that Earth's climate is getting warmer much faster than during any other time in its history. The amount of carbon dioxide in the atmosphere is increasing too. A warmer climate can affect many systems on Earth.

☑ Reading Check **Compare and Contrast**
Compare and contrast the changes caused by ash from volcanoes and carbon dioxide from fires.

_____

_____

_____

_____

INTERACTIVITY

Complete an activity about climate changes.

☑ Lesson 2 Check

1. **Infer** How is the climate of Earth changing?

_____

2. **Analyze** How do human activities change climate?

_____

_____

How do changing glaciers show climate change?

Materials
• ruler

Glaciers are made up of snow that is pressed together to form ice over many, many years. How might changes in glaciers help scientists study climate change?

Science Practice

Scientists obtain and combine information from various sources to explain natural processes.

Procedure

☐ **1.** Predict how you think a change in climate would affect a glacier.

_____

_____

_____

☐ **2.** The different colored lines on the glacier photo show where the glacier ended in a specific year. Use the ruler and the photo to collect data about the length of the glacier in each of the given years. Record your measurements.

Year	Length of glacier
1950	
1974	
2006	
2011	

Analyze and Interpret Data

3. **CCC Patterns** What pattern do you see in your measurements?

_____

_____

4. **Draw Conclusions** What change in climate do you think is causing the change to the glacier that you observed?

_____

_____

5. **Apply** How could you use glaciers to show climate change in your movie?

_____

_____

_____

100 Meters

1950
1974
2006
2011

⬇ **INTERACTIVITY**

Go online to see how climate change can affect home gardens.

Climate Change in a Bottle

Phenomenon Engineers use models to investigate complicated problems and processes. Earth's climate change is a complicated process, so models are a good way to investigate it.

To make climate models, scientists and engineers review data that have been gathered about Earth's climate in the past. They also look carefully at information about the processes that affect Earth's climate. Then they build computer programs to analyze the information and make predictions.

Model It

You can use a few common materials to make a simple model of how greenhouse gases in the atmosphere can affect climate. You can use two clear, plastic jars, one lid, some soil, two thermometers, a lamp, and some water.

☐ Draw a plan to make two models. One model will not show the greenhouse effect. The other model will show the greenhouse effect on climate. In both models, the jars represent the atmosphere.

☐ What data will you collect to show that the greenhouse effect changes climate?

_____

☐ Show your plan to your teacher. Then build your models. Record your data.

World Climates

LOCAL-TO-GLOBAL Connection

You may know that our country does not have just one climate. The southwest part of the country is hot and dry. The southeast is hot and humid. The northwest is generally cool and rainy. Cold winters are common in the northern midwest.

The United States and China spread across similar latitudes. For that reason, they have some climates that are alike. For example, the Chinese city of Harbin has very cold winters like Portland, Maine. Guangzhou has hot summers, warm winters, and a lot of rain like New Orleans, Louisiana.

Describe Where in China would you likely find a city with a climate similar to the climate where you live?

_____

_____

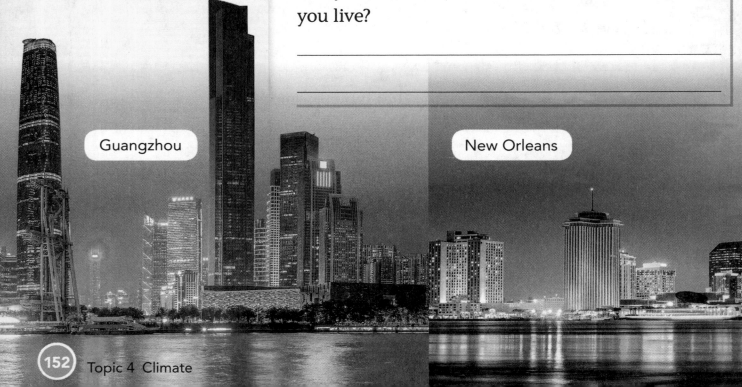

Guangzhou

New Orleans

How do **mountains** affect climate?

One way to understand how mountains affect climate is to make a model. How can you use a model to observe what happens when clouds move toward a mountain?

Materials

- small electric fan
- cotton balls
- obstacles (books, chairs, boxes)
- goggles

Science Practice

Scientists use models to explain natural processes.

⚠ Be careful using the fan.
⚠ Wear safety goggles.

Procedure

☐ 1. **SEP Develop a Model** Plan a model to show what happens to clouds when they move toward a mountain. Use all of the materials. Identify which materials represent clouds and which represent mountains.

☐ 2. **SEP Use a Model** Show your plan to your teacher before you begin. Record your observations.

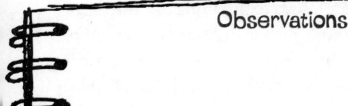

Observations

Analyze and Interpret Data

3. **SEP Explain** How can mountains affect climate? Use evidence from your investigation to make your explanation.

_____

_____

_____

Dry Climates

The pictures show two places with different kinds of climate. They get different amounts of precipitation each year. Scientists use precipitation and temperature to **classify**, or make groups of, climates.

Places that get little rain or snow have dry climates. The most familiar places with dry climates are deserts. Deserts have an **arid**, or very dry, climate. They get less than 25 centimeters (9 inches) of rain each year. The plants in a desert can store water. They use this water during long periods with no rain. Many people think of deserts as hot places. But some deserts are very cold. Most of Antarctica is a cold desert. No plants grow in the Antarctic desert.

Other dry climates have enough rain for short grasses and small bushes to grow. These areas have more water than a desert but not enough for forests to grow. The Great Plains in the center of the United States has this type of dry climate. Many areas in Africa, Asia, and South America also have this type of climate.

Infer Plants are often far away from one another in a desert. Why do you think this is so?

_____

_____

_____

Wet Climates

Scientists classify wet climates by temperature. Tropical climates are found in the warmest parts of Earth, near the equator. Plants grow quickly in tropical climates. Places with a tropical climate often have dense forests.

Places in the middle of continents north or south of the tropical zones have temperate continental climates. These places have hot summers. Winters are cool or cold. Temperate marine climates are located near coastal areas. The climates in these places are milder than the temperate continental climates.

Places with polar climates are very cold in the winter. Even in the middle of summer, the temperature usually stays below 10 °C (50 °F). No trees grow in polar climate zones. Smaller plants grow very quickly in the summer. In some places, the soil below the surface stays frozen all year.

Identify Why do you think climates are milder along coastal areas?

_____

_____

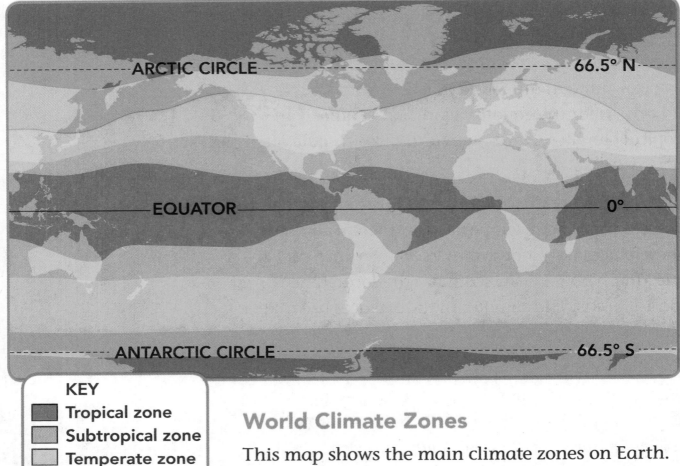

Map labels: ARCTIC CIRCLE · 66.5° N · EQUATOR · 0° · ANTARCTIC CIRCLE · 66.5° S

KEY
- Tropical zone
- Subtropical zone
- Temperate zone
- Subpolar zone
- Polar zone

World Climate Zones

This map shows the main climate zones on Earth. Find these five main types of climate.

- *Tropical zone* The weather is hot and humid all year.

- *Subtropical zone* Summers here are hot. Winters are mild to cool.

- *Temperate zone* Summers are hot to very warm. Winters are cold.

- *Subpolar zone* Summers are short with cold or mild temperatures. Winters are long and very cold.

- *Polar zone* Temperatures are cool to very cold all year.

Question It!

Certain kinds of grass have roots that grow more than 2 meters (7 feet) below the surface. What question could you ask to find out in which climate zone these grasses are likely to grow?

_____

_____

_____

_____

⬇ **INTERACTIVITY**

Complete an activity about climate changes.

Crosscutting Concepts ▸ Toolbox

Patterns Scientists study patterns to understand how things are related. Look at the continents on the climate map. What patterns can you find in the locations of different climate types on the continents?

☑ **READING CHECK** **Compare and Contrast**

What is the main difference between a tropical climate and a polar climate? How are they similar?

_____

_____

_____

_____

Quest Connection

Suppose your movie has many scenes with snow. In which climate zone would you film your movie? Why?

_____

_____

_____

_____

Climate Extremes

Would you like to live in a place where the average winter temperature is –50 °C (–58 °F)? That is what the winter temperatures are in Oymyakon, Russia. The remote village is generally considered the coldest area on Earth where people live. In contrast, the average summer temperature in Death Valley, United States, is 45 °C (113 °F). The highest temperature recorded was 57 °C (134 °F). Mountains along the coast prevent precipitation from reaching the valley. The shape of the valley prevents hot air from leaving. These factors and the intense sun make Death Valley very hot.

📓 **Write About It** In your science notebook, describe what you think living in one of these extreme temperatures would be like. How would you deal with the extreme cold or heat?

☑ Lesson 3 Check

1. **Identify** What are two categories of data that can help you determine the climate of an area?

   temperature and precipition

2. **Analyze** Why might places that are at the same latitude in different parts of the world have different climates?

   they have clevation

Explore the World

Think about the action that will take place in the movie. The scenes will be filmed in at least three different places.

The table shows cities you can think about using for some of the scenes. The information for some cities is filled in. Use the Internet or another source approved by your teacher to obtain information and complete the table.

Location	Continent	Latitude	Type of climate
Edmonton, Canada	North America	53.5° N	Subpolar
Barcelona, Spain	Europe	41.4° N	Temperate
Moscow, Russia	Asia	55.8° N	Subpolar
Geneva, Switzerland	Europe	46.2° N	Temperate
Salta, Argentina			
Tokyo, Japan			
Watamu, Kenya			
Savissivik, Greenland			

Draw Conclusions Compare your table with a partner's. Then take turns describing climates in each location. Decide which locations would be best to include in the movie.

Quest Findings

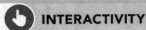

Climates on Location
Where should we film a movie?

Identify the Scenes

Phenomenon As a location scout, you need to find locations for your movie scenes. Describe three outdoor scenes in the movie. Then describe climates that have weather conditions that are appropriate for each scene. Finally, choose a city from the Lesson 3 Check-In for each scene.

Scene	Climate	City

Present Your Findings

Make a short presentation explaining why each location is best for each scene.

Movie Location Scout

How would you like to be the first person on the scene of a new movie? If so, maybe you want to be a movie location scout. The scout is the person who decides where the movie will be made. What would you do if that was your job? First, you have to read the script carefully. You need to know exactly what is in the scene. Then you make a list of places that have the things the movie needs. For the outdoor scene, you have to consider weather. You may need to find an unused beach or a dense forest. After choosing the location, the scout then has to work out details with the owner of the land. The scout is present during filming to help solve any problems about the location.

📓 **Write About It** Do you think you would enjoy being a location scout? Explain why you think so in your science notebook.

1. **Vocabulary** What is the main difference between the weather at a place and its climate?

   A. Climate can change, but the weather is always the same.

   B. Weather describes conditions at one time, but climate is a pattern over a long time.

   C. Weather is a measure of temperature, but climate is a measure of precipitation.

   D. Weather does not affect living things in an area, but climate does affect them.

2. **Use Diagrams** How can a tall mountain have several different climates?

   _____

   _____

   _____

   _____

3. **Explain** Temperate climates generally are much warmer in summer than in winter. What causes this seasonal difference?

   A. Earth is closer to the sun in summer than in winter.

   B. Temperate areas get more direct sunlight in summer than in winter.

   C. Winds generally blow from the ocean in summer and toward the ocean in winter.

   D. There are fewer clouds to block sunlight in the summer.

4. **Infer** Too much carbon dioxide can cause the climates of Earth to become warmer. What would happen if there were no greenhouse gases at all?

   A. Earth's climate would stay the same.

   B. Earth would become cooler.

   C. Earth would become warmer.

   D. The climate would become warmer near the equator and cooler near the poles.

5. Evaluate a Plan An engineer plans to build a taller smokestack. It will release the carbon dioxide that comes from burning fuel higher in the atmosphere. The engineer thinks this change will reduce the greenhouse effect of carbon dioxide. Is this plan likely to work? Explain your answer.

_____

_____

_____

_____

6. Use Evidence Before agriculture, a large part of the country of Argentina was a grassland called the Pampas. The Pampas has many types of grasses and small shrubs. It has few trees. What is the climate of the Pampas?

A. dry

B. polar

C. temperate continental

D. tropical rainy

The Essential Question

How can you explain what climate is like in different places?

Show What You Learned

One factor that causes climates to vary in different places is latitude. All of the places at one latitude receive the same amount of sunlight. Places at the same latitude can have very different climates, though. Why would two places at the same latitude have different climates?

_____

_____

_____

_____

_____

_____

_____

_____

_____

_____

_____

This map shows some climate areas of the United States. Students studied the map and drew conclusions based on their knowledge of climate. The students then used the Internet to find temperature and precipitation data for two cities.

Climates in Two Cities			
City	Average January high temp	Average July high temp	Average yearly precipitation
Grand Forks	-9°C (16°F)	27°C (81°F)	56 cm
Seattle	8°C (46°F)	24°C (75°F)	94 cm

KEY
- Cold/Very Cold
- Mixed-Humid
- Hot-Humid
- Hot-Dry/Mixed-Dry
- Marine

1. **Evaluate** Climate zones tend to get warmer from the top part of the map to the bottom part. What would cause this pattern of climates in the states? Explain your answer.

_____

_____

_____

_____

2. **Cause and Effect** Both cities on the map are located at about the same latitude. What factor is most responsible for the differences in their climates?

   A. The climate in Seattle is warmer and wetter because it is close to the ocean.

   B. The climate in Grand Forks is colder and drier because it is farther from the equator.

   C. Seattle has a milder climate because there are many more plants growing there that capture solar energy.

   D. Grand Forks has a more variable climate because it is located in an area with mountains.

3. **Explain** Two places in the middle of the western part of the country have colder climates than the area around them. What factor is likely to cause this difference in climate?

_____

_____

_____

_____

4. **Interpret** Which climate zone in the United States is likely to have the fewest number and types of plants growing there?

   A. The area along the coast with a marine climate.

   B. The area in the southeastern part of the country with a hot-humid climate.

   C. The area in the middle of the country with a cold climate.

   D. The area in the southwest with a hot-dry climate.

uDemonstrate Lab

What affects the climate in a region?

Phenomenon Scientists combine different kinds of information to explain something. In this activity, you will come up with an imaginary place on Earth. How can you figure out what type of climate it would have?

Materials
• sheet of paper
• colored pencils
• ruler

Suggested Materials
• Internet access

Procedure

☐ **1.** Brainstorm ideas for the location of a made-up city. Include features that would affect the city's climate, such as mountains or an ocean.

_____

_____

_____

_____

Science Practice

Scientists _combine information_ from multiple sources to explain natural phenomena.

☐ **2.** Describe the climate characteristics of the city. Identify the type of climate the city has.

_____

_____

_____

_____

☐ **3.** On a sheet of paper, draw a map of your city and the area around it. Show the features you identified in step 1. Also include the latitude of your city.

☐ **4.** Exchange maps with another group. Use information on the map to describe the climate of their city.

Analyze and Interpret Data

5. Interpret Did you correctly describe the climate in the map of the other group? What features of the map helped you? How?

_____

_____

_____

_____

6. Communicate How did making a map and analyzing it help you understand that the climate of a place depends on more than one factor?

_____

_____

_____

_____

_____

Life Cycles and Traits

Lesson 1 Life Cycles

Lesson 2 Inherited Traits

Lesson 3 Traits Influenced by the Environment

Next Generation Science Standards

3-LS1-1 Develop models to describe that organisms have unique and diverse life cycles but all have in common birth, growth, reproduction, and death.

3-LS3-1 Analyze and interpret data to provide evidence that plants and animals have traits inherited from parents and that variation of these traits exists in a group of similar organisms.

3-LS3-2 Use evidence to support the explanation that traits can be influenced by the environment.

▶ VIDEO

📖 eTEXT

👆 INTERACTIVITY

📱 VIRTUAL LAB

🎮 GAME

☑ ASSESSMENT

The Essential Question
How do the traits of living things vary?

Show What You Know

How are these tulips the same and different?

_____

_____

_____

_____

STEM Design a
Mystery Creature

How are living things suited to their environments?

Phenomenon Greetings! I am Rida Ai, an ecologist. I have been contacted by a movie company. They want help to design animals and plants that would live in a mystery location.

In this problem-based learning activity, you will learn about the mysterious place. You will investigate how the environment affects the things that live there, and what traits help the living things survive. You can help me describe what kinds of plants or animals would be found.

Follow the path to learn how you will complete the Quest. The Quest activities in the lessons will help you complete the Quest! Check off your progress on the path when you complete an activity with a QUEST CHECK ✔ OFF . Go online for more Quest activities.

Quest Check-In Lab 1

Lesson 1

Look at information about an environment. Analyze what kinds of animals can live there.

Next Generation Science Standards

3-LS3-1 Analyze and interpret data to provide evidence that plants and animals have traits inherited from parents and that variation of these traits exists in a group of similar organisms. **3-LS3-2** Use evidence to support the explanation that traits can be influenced by the environment.

Quest Check-In 3

Lesson 3

Give advice to the set designer about how to grow the best plants.

Quest Check-In 2

Lesson 2

Explore how animals can blend into their environments.

Quest Findings

Complete the Quest! Draw or describe a plant or animal that would likely survive in the mystery environment.

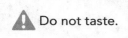
Which seeds are from which plant?

Scientists collect, analyze, and interpret data to help develop an argument for how to group organisms. How can you develop an argument based on evidence for which seeds are from the same type of plant?

Materials
- ruler
- assorted seeds
- graph paper

⚠ Do not taste.

Procedure

☐ **1.** Make a plan for how you will collect, analyze, and interpret data about the seeds. Use the materials. Show your plan to your teacher before you begin.

☐ **2.** Record your observations in a table on a separate sheet of paper.

Science Practice

Scientists analyze data to find relationships among things.

Analyze and Interpret Data

3. SEP Interpret Data How many different types of seeds were in your sample?

_____

_____

_____

4. SEP Use Evidence How did you know which seeds belonged to a certain kind of plant?

_____

_____

_____

_____

Use Text Features

When you read for information, you can use text features, such as photos, art, or maps, to help you understand the text better. You can often get information in the features that is not stated in the text. Read about cichlid fish.

GAME

Practice what you learn with the Mini Games.

So Many Fish

The lakes in Africa's Rift Valley are home to many unique ecosystems. An incredible variety of fish live there. Most of these fish are cichlids. All cichlids share some traits, but each of the many different kinds of cichlids in these lakes also has its own traits. Shape is one of them. Some cichlids are shaped like a tube. Some are flat. They have other shapes too. Cichlids are enjoyed by many people with aquariums. Their common behaviors make them interesting fish to watch.

☑ READING CHECK **Use Text Features** What differences in the traits of cichlids can you see in the photos?

_____

_____

_____

_____

Life Cycles

I can...

Describe how all life cycles follow the same pattern.

3-LS1-1

Literacy Skill
Use Text Features

Vocabulary
organism
reproduce

Academic Vocabulary
diverse

▶ **VIDEO**

Watch a video about life cycles.

ENGINEERING Connection

Leatherback sea turtles are named for their soft, leathery shells. These turtles live in the ocean for most of the year. However, mother turtles return to the beach to lay their eggs. They dig nests in the sand with their rear flippers. Each turtle lays her eggs, covers them, and returns to the ocean. After two months, the eggs begin to hatch. At night, the baby turtles crawl toward the ocean.

Young turtles have a small chance that they will get to the ocean. Predators will capture many of them. Some will be confused by bright lights near the beach. Engineers and concerned citizens are working together to find ways to help the baby turtles. Barriers and signs in some places keep the baby turtles safe.

📓 **Write About It** In your science notebook, write about what you think it would be like to watch baby sea turtles hatch and crawl toward the ocean at night.

How are life cycles similar and different?

Scientists investigate to find out how organisms are alike and different. How can you compare life cycles?

Procedure

☐ **1.** Use the Life Cycles sheet to observe how life cycles are alike and different.

☐ **2. SEP Develop Models** Plan a way to make a model that shows how life cycles are alike and different. You can use any of the materials. Include both plants and animals in your model.

☐ **3.** Show your plan to your teacher before you begin.

☐ **4. SEP Use Models** After you complete your model, trade with another group. Discuss the similarities and differences in life cycles that the models show.

 Be careful with scissors.

Science Practice

Scientists use models to describe phenomena.

Analyze and Interpret Data

5. CCC Systems and Models How does your model and the other group's model show that life cycles are alike? How do they show that life cycles are different?

_____

_____

_____

_____

_____

Diversity of Living Things

Earth has millions of different kinds of organisms. An **organism** is a living thing, such as a plant or an animal. You are an organism too! The sprouting plant and the newborn elk in the photos are just two of the diverse kinds of organisms on Earth. **Diverse** means that there are many different kinds.

Although organisms are diverse, they are alike in some ways. Each organism begins life, grows, and dies. All kinds of organisms also reproduce. When an organism **reproduces**, it makes more organisms of the same kind as the parent. Living things reproduce so that organisms of their kind can continue to live on Earth.

Compare In what ways is the newborn elk like its mother?

_____

_____

_____

Plant Reproduction

Organisms can begin their life in different ways. We usually think of a seed as the beginning of life for a plant. Seeds come in many different sizes, shapes, and colors. But all seeds have the same parts.

The outside part protects the plant. Inside the seed is a tiny plant. Under the right conditions, the seed can sprout. The seed needs air, the right temperature, and the right amount of water to sprout. The seed has stored food that the tiny plant uses when it starts to grow into a new plant.

The picture shows a sunflower seed that has begun to sprout. The green part will become the stem and leaves. Roots will grow downward from the seed. Soon the new plant will be able to make its own food.

Identify What are the three main parts of a seed?

_____

_____

u Be a Scientist

Observing Growth
With an adult, fill a clear plastic cup with soil. Plant a bean against the side of the cup. In a notebook, record your observations as the plant grows.

Question It!

Suppose you wanted to sprout the seeds of a particular kind of plant. What questions would you ask before you planted the seeds?

_____

_____

_____

_____

_____

Animal Reproduction

Most animals start as an egg. Some animals start life as an egg that is so small that you can barely see it. Others produce eggs that are easy to see. Some of these animals lay eggs outside their body. The bird eggs in the photo are very different sizes. The largest one is from an ostrich, whose eggs are the largest among birds' eggs. Can you tell the size of the birds that laid the other eggs?

Different animals have different ways of protecting their eggs. Bird eggs have a hard covering that protects the young birds inside. The fish in the photo carries eggs in its mouth! Unlike the bird's egg, these eggs do not have a hard covering. The eggs will stay in the parent's mouth until they hatch. Until they do, the parent cannot eat.

Life Cycles

When an animal lays eggs outside of its body, the young animal grows inside the eggs. The egg hatches when the young animal is ready to come out. The ostrich in the photo is coming out of its egg because it is too big for its shell.

For most mammals, the egg starts developing into a young animal inside the mother's body. When the young animal is the right size, it is born.

Young animals, such as elephants, sometimes stay with their parents after they are born. They leave their parents when they can take care of themselves. Other animals do not stay with their young at all. Most fish lay their eggs and then leave them. The young fish must take care of themselves.

☑ READING CHECK **Use Text Features** How does the green text in this lesson help you understand the lesson?

_____

_____

Quest Connection

▼▼▼▼▼▼▼▼▼▼▼▼▼▼▼▼▼▼▼▼▼▼▼▼▼▼▼▼▼▼

Think about the animals on these pages. How is the start of their life similar? How is it different?

_____

_____

_____

_____

How are life cycles the same?

All living things go through a life cycle. The ant, the polar bear, and the pea plant are different organisms but go through similar stages in their life cycles.

Red Ant

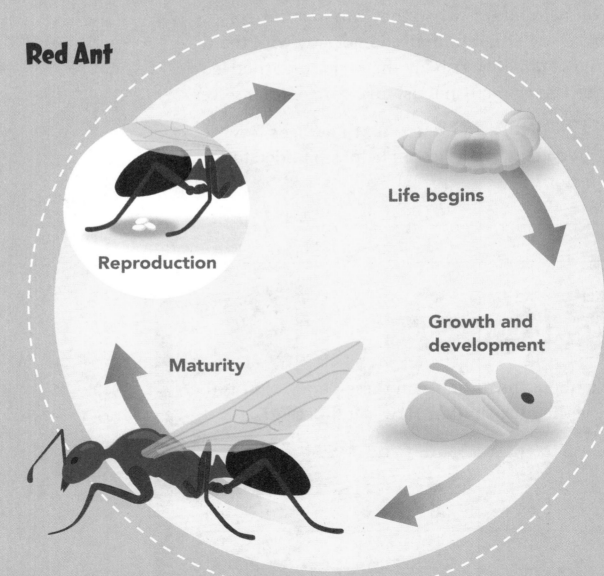

Reproduction

Life begins

Growth and development

Maturity

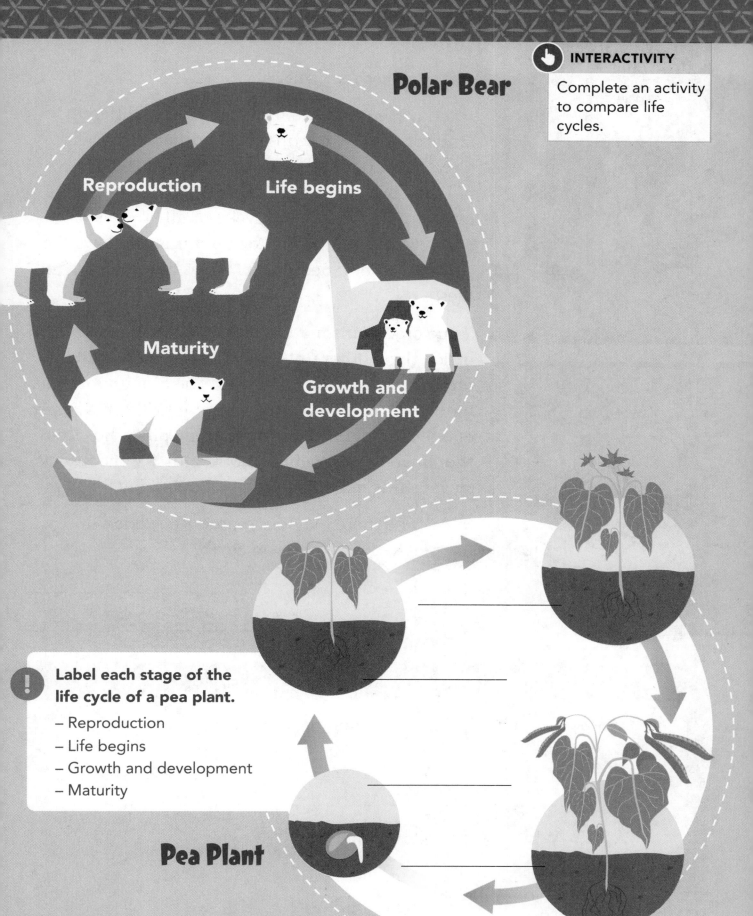

Polar Bear

Reproduction

Life begins

Maturity

Growth and development

INTERACTIVITY

Complete an activity to compare life cycles.

Label each stage of the life cycle of a pea plant.

– Reproduction
– Life begins
– Growth and development
– Maturity

Pea Plant

Pattern of Life Cycles

You have learned how the life cycles of different kinds of organisms can be very different. When a red ant is born, it does not look similar to its parents. But a polar bear looks almost the same as its parent. Yet the life cycles of all organisms are alike in some ways. Each organism follows the same pattern. It begins life, grows, reproduces, and dies.

Some organisms hatch from an egg. Others develop inside the mother until they are born. Each kind of organism also grows and dies. The amount of time for growth can be very different. A California forest of one kind of tree—the bristlecone pine—has trees that have lived for about 5,000 years! Some insects, such as this mayfly, live only about a day.

Infer If no more mayflies reproduce, what will happen to the mayflies on Earth?

_____

_____

☑ Lesson 1 Check

1. Summarize What is the pattern for all life cycles?

_____

_____

2. Explain Why is reproduction important?

_____

_____

_____

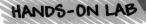
Which animals can live here?

Animals must get what they need to survive from their environment. Can these organisms live in the same environment?

Materials
- Animals sheet
- scissors

⚠ Be careful using scissors.

Science Practice

Scientists *interpret data* they collect in order to understand what it means.

Procedure

☐ **1.** Cut out the pictures of the animals from the Animals sheet. Make observations to identify the needs of the organisms. Match the young organism with its adult.

☐ **2.** Look at the picture of the environment. Identify the animals that could live in the environment.

Analyze and Interpret Data

3. SEP Interpret Data Can this environment support all of the animals during their entire life cycle? Explain why not for each animal that could not live there.

_____

_____

_____

_____

Lesson 2

Inherited Traits

I can...

Explain that living things inherit many characteristics from their parents. Provide evidence showing that traits vary in a group of similar organisms.

3-LS3-1

Literacy Skill
Use Text Features

Vocabulary
trait
inherit

Academic Vocabulary
variation

▶ **VIDEO**

Watch a video about inherited traits.

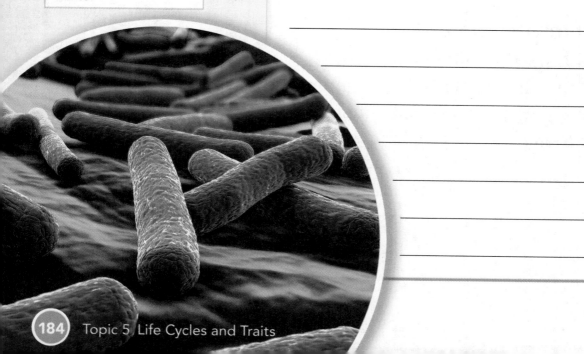

STEM ⟩ Connection

Insulin is something the human body usually makes. It helps keep the right amount of sugar in a person's blood. The bodies of some people do not make enough insulin. Those people need to take insulin as a medicine. The insulin they take is made by bacteria.

Although some bacteria cause illness, most are harmless or even helpful. All organisms, including bacteria, have coded instructions that help make offspring similar to parents. Scientists can change these instructions through a process called genetic engineering. The process allows scientists to make bacteria that produce insulin.

Infer Can the offspring of the genetically engineered bacteria make insulin? Explain your answer.

_____

_____

_____

_____

_____

_____

How do offspring compare to their PARENTS?

Materials
• Raccoon Footprints sheet
• metric ruler

Scientists look for patterns in the features of related organisms. What differences can you find in the footprints of a family of raccoons?

Procedure

Science Practice

Scientists analyze data to look for patterns.

☐ **1.** Use the materials to collect data on the footprints of a family of raccoons.

☐ **2.** Record your observations.

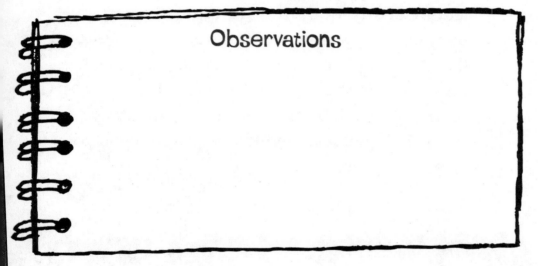

Observations

Analyze and Interpret Data

3. SEP Analyze How were the footprints similar? How were they different? Use data to support your answer.

_____

_____

_____

Traits from Parents

You can tell that the puppies in the picture are the same kind of dog. They have many features that are similar. For example, the fur is the same colors.

✓ **READING CHECK** **Use Text Features** What other ways can you see in the photo that the puppies are alike?

_____

_____

The reason that the puppies are so much alike is that they got their traits from their parents. A **trait** is a feature of an organism. A trait can be the way the body of the organism looks or works. It can also be the things the organism does. For example, some animals know how to walk and feed themselves as soon as they are born. These actions are inherited traits. To **inherit** something means that you got it from your parents or ancestors.

Traits of Parents and Offspring

Offspring of the same parents have similar inherited traits. Offspring usually look a little like their mother and a little like their father. But they do not look exactly like either parent. That is why the puppies have some differences. The differences in organisms from the same parent is called **variation**.

Compare and Contrast The parents of the puppies are black and white, just as the puppies are. In what other ways are the puppies similar to their parents? How are they different?

_____

_____

_____

_____

_____

_____

пBe a Scientist

Identify Traits
Choose a type of plant or animal in your area. Observe at least 10 individuals. Record how their traits are alike or different.

Question It! Suppose you found an animal that was a very unusual color. What are two questions you could ask to learn whether the trait could be inherited?

_____

_____

_____

_____

_____

Traits in Similar Plants

The plants in the photos do not come from the same parent plants. They are, though, the same kind of plant—pea plants. Their flowers and leaves have the same shape. Most pea plants have leaves and flowers with these same shapes. But the flowers of the two plants are different colors. Plants of the same kind have variations in their traits.

Color is not the only way plants vary. The red and orange flowers are all the same kind. Yet some of the plants are taller than others. Plants of the same kind have other variations, such as small differences in leaf shape and color, the number of thorns on a stem, or how rough a tree's bark is.

Make Meaning You are the same kind of organism as all the people around you. In your science notebook, tell how you are unique. List ways you are different from other people.

Traits in Similar Animals

One reason people like to collect shells is that shells come in many sizes, shapes, colors, and patterns. Some of the differences are because the shells are from different kinds of animals. The snail shells in the picture, though, are the same kind of animal—the white-lipped banded snail. Like plants, animals of the same kind have variations in their traits.

INTERACTIVITY

Complete an activity about traits and offspring.

Quest Connection

Suppose the shells in the photo fell from the plant stem into some sand. Which shells would be easiest to see? Why?

_____

_____

_____

☑ Lesson 2 Check

1. **Explain** Two black cats produced kittens with black fur. Why did the kittens have black fur?

_____

_____

2. **Identify** Give an example of how traits vary in a group of organisms of the same kind.

_____

_____

Hide Me

The mystery environment will probably have predators and prey. Camouflage, or blending in with the surroundings, is one way that animals survive. Animals with the best camouflage are more likely to survive. By blending in with the surroundings, prey animals can avoid being eaten. Predators can use camouflage to hide from their prey until they are ready to strike. Draw a line from each animal to the environment where it could be best camouflaged.

Mammal Eggs?

The duck-billed platypus is extreme for more than one reason. It uses its bill to sense electricity. Males produce poison, which is rare among mammals. Females release milk through the skin on their bellies. Perhaps their most unusual feature, though, is that they are mammals that lay eggs!

Mammals are warm-blooded animals, with bones. Scientists think that ancient ancestors of mammals laid eggs. But that was many millions of years ago. Today nearly all mammals give live birth. The platypus, however, has inherited the ancient trait of laying eggs. The only other mammals that lay eggs are echidnas. Echidnas are closely related to the platypus.

How does a platypus provide evidence that traits can vary among similar animals?

_____

_____

_____

▶ **VIDEO**

Watch a video about genetic engineering of plants.

A Fruitful Change

Phenomenon What do you think an engineer helps to build? Most people probably think of big projects such as bridges or towers. But some engineers make things too small to see. Genetic engineering is a way of using technology to change the traits of an organism. Scientists have used genetic engineering to make fruits that ripen more slowly. They have modified plants so that they can resist pests that eat them. They have made tomatoes that are bigger and last longer. Genetic engineering has many useful purposes.

Define It

It is time to make a better plant. You are a genetic engineer! Choose a fruit or vegetable that someone might buy at a grocery store. How can you make the fruit or vegetable better?

☐ What fruit or vegetable would you like to improve?

_____

☐ What are some traits of the fruit or vegetable?

_____

_____

☐ Which trait would you like to improve? Why?

_____

_____

_____

_____

☐ Define the problem you will solve with genetic engineering. Tell what trait you will change. Describe the new, improved trait.

_____

_____

_____

_____

_____

_____

_____

Lesson 3
Traits Influenced by the Environment

SPORTS ▸ Connection

Chance was an active dog. She enjoyed playing fetch, running around outside, and chasing other dog friends. She even took part in dog shows. Chance survived a bad accident, but could not use her hind legs. During recovery, Chance was not able to be active. Without activity, Chance gained weight. This caused the veterinarian to worry about the pup's health. The family that Chance lived with got help to make a special cart to allow her to run again. With wheels on the back, Chance could once again play fetch and run around. People no longer needed to worry about her weight.

Identify What trait of the dog was affected and caused concern?

How can the environment affect an organism?

Yeasts are living things that are related to mushrooms. They live in moist places. They need sugar to stay alive and reproduce. How can differences in an environment affect yeasts?

Procedure

☐ 1. **SEP Plan an Investigation** Make a plan to investigate how differences in the environment can affect the growth of yeasts. Use all the materials. Identify the variable you will test and control all other variables.

☐ 2. Show your plan to your teacher before you begin. Record your observations.

Materials
- safety goggles
- warm water
- graduated cylinder
- plastic cups
- vinegar
- spoon
- yeast
- clock
- sugar

⚠ Wear safety goggles.
⚠ Do not taste.

Science Practice

Scientists use evidence to make explanations.

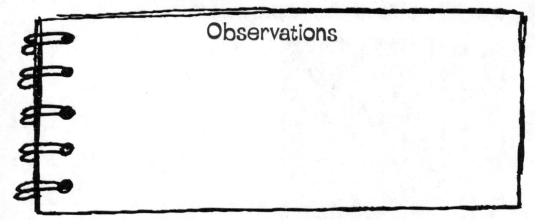

Observations

Analyze and Interpret Data

3. **SEP Engage in Argument from Evidence** Can the environment affect living things? Use evidence from your data to support your answer.

_____

_____

_____

Crosscutting Concepts ▸ Toolbox

Cause and Effect
Scientists look for patterns in nature that show cause and effect. What is the cause-and-effect relationship that saguaro cactuses show?

Inherited Traits and the Environment

The pictures show two different saguaro cactuses. Saguaro cactuses are usually tall with one main stem. Some saguaros branch out, while others do not. Why are their shapes so different?

Scientists studied the growth patterns of saguaro cactuses. They found that these plants form more branches when the environment has more water.

Many of the traits of a saguaro cactus are inherited from the parents. These include its shape. But the environment also affects the shape of the cactus. The amount of water makes the difference.

Infer Which photo shows an environment that probably has more water?

_____
_____
_____
_____
_____
_____
_____
_____

Environmental Factors

As you just learned, the amount of water in the environment can affect inherited traits of the cactus. This is because the environment can **influence**, or have an effect on, inherited traits.

Water is just one factor in the environment that can influence inherited traits. Other factors include the kind and amount of food, the temperature, the kind of soil, and the materials in the soil, air, and water.

The flowers in the picture are hydrangeas. Their color can be blue or pink. The color depends on the kind of soil the plant grows in.

☑ **READING CHECK** **Use Text Features** How does the highlighted vocabulary word help you as you read the text?

_____

_____

_____

👆 **INTERACTIVITY**

Complete an activity about how the environment affects traits.

Quest Connection

What parts of the environment could you change to get bigger plants?

_____

_____

How can environmental factors affect organisms?

Factors in an organism's environment can affect traits of the organism.

> ! For each organism, circle the environmental factor you think causes the change in its traits.

A flamingo's feathers are actually white.

The feathers turn pink when a flamingo eats shrimp and algae, which contain carotene.

The temperature that surrounds a nest of crocodile eggs can influence whether the crocodile becomes a male or female.

Leaf size in the holly oak changes with temperature. When the environment is warmer, the leaves grow larger.

When the water flea moves through its life cycle, it can develop a longer tail and helmet-like protection for its head. The protective body parts help the water flea survive when predators are near.

No predators nearby.

Predators are close.

Sunlight and Plant Traits

Sunlight is an important factor that affects the traits of plants. In the photo, the plant on the left shows how this plant grows when it has the right amount of sunlight. The plant in the middle did not get enough sunlight. The plant on the right got sunlight only from one side.

Explain What inherited trait of this plant does sunlight influence?

_____

☑ Lesson 3 Check

1. **Explain** How can the environment affect the height of a tree?

_____

_____

2. **Identify** What evidence from the text supports the conclusion that traits can be influenced by the environment?

_____

_____

Set the Scene

The set designer for the movie wants to include large, healthy, colorful flowers in the mystery location. He wants to use lupines such as the ones in the photo.

What environmental factors should the designer consider for the location? Write the factors in the table.

How can each factor affect the lupines? Write the effects in the table.

Factor	Effect

Write a short message to the set designer explaining what the environment must be like in the mystery location to grow such beautiful lupines.

_____

_____

_____

INTERACTIVITY

Organize data to support your Quest Findings.

STEM Design a Mystery Creature

How are living things suited to their environments?

Phenomenon Read the description of the mystery movie location. Then use your knowledge to describe an imaginary animal or plant character that would likely survive there. The movie company will use the description to make a character for the movie.

Mystery Location Features

- **Average summer temperature:** 18°C (65°F)

- **Average winter temperature:** 0°C (32°F)

- **Average summer precipitation:** very rainy

- **Average winter precipitation:** extremely rainy

- **Amount of sunlight:** sunlight in winter; shady most of the summer

- **Other features:** dense forests and bogs with many streams and lakes

Draw a picture or write a description of the imaginary character that could survive in these conditions. Explain how its features will help it survive in the environment.

QUEST CHECK ✓ OFF

Ecologist

Ecologists are scientists who study how living things interact with each other and their environment. They study how the environment affects living things.

Ecologists spend a lot of time working outdoors. They sometimes work in labs, as well.

Ecologists need a college degree. They need to know how to design a scientific study. They must be good at math. They are also experts on different kinds of organisms. If you like working outdoors and you want to understand nature, you might make a great ecologist.

> 📓 **Make Meaning**
> What are some kinds of observations an ecologist might make? In your science notebook, write about several different kinds of things you would like to observe if you were an ecologist.

1. **Make Generalizations** What are the four stages of a life cycle pattern that all organisms share?

   _____

   _____

   _____

   _____

   _____

2. **Develop a Model** Sujin wants to model the life cycle of a mammal. Which choice describes how she should build the model?

   A. construct a time line starting at birth and ending at death

   B. construct a pyramid showing what the animal eats throughout its life

   C. construct a circular diagram showing only growth and death

   D. construct a Venn diagram showing how a mammal's life is similar to another organism's

3. Which statement best explains why crows have black feathers?

   A. Their parents had black feathers.

   B. The color makes it easier for predators to see them.

   C. Black feathers are the best looking.

   D. They need black feathers to fly.

4. **Apply Concepts** Which of these is an example of how the environment influences a trait?

   A. Unlike dogs, the claws of cats can be pulled back inside the paw.

   B. A squirrel visits the same bird feeder each day to look for food.

   C. A chameleon changes color to match the color of its surroundings.

   D. In a year with very little rain, a fruit tree produces fruit that is smaller than usual.

Use the photo to answer questions 5 and 6.

5. **Compare and Contrast** Identify one way these animals are alike and one way they are different.

Alike

_____

_____

Different

_____

_____

6. **Identify** Write one example of an inherited trait that you can see in the photo.

_____

7. **Summarize** How are offspring similar to and different from their parents?

_____

_____

_____

How do the traits of living things vary?

Show What You Learned
Choose an example organism.

- Explain how inherited traits vary for this organism.
- Explain how the environment influences the traits of this organism.

_____

_____

_____

_____

_____

_____

_____

_____

_____

_____

_____

_____

_____

_____

The chart shows information about traits in a family of cats. Look at the chart, and then answer the questions.

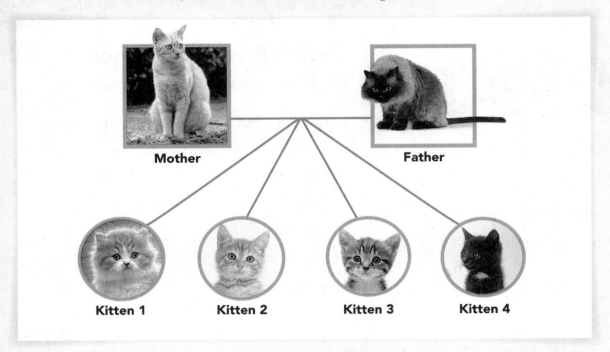

1. **Infer** What can you infer about fur color in this family of cats?

   A. Fur color is determined by the environment.

   B. Fur color is random and cannot be predicted.

   C. Fur color does not change when it is inherited.

   D. Fur color is a trait that is inherited and can vary.

2. **Observe Patterns** Describe the pattern of traits you can observe in this family.

   _____

   _____

   _____

   _____

3. **Interpret Data** The adult cats have sets of traits that are different from any of the kittens. Why do the kittens not have the same traits as the parents?

_____

_____

_____

_____

4. **Interpret Data** All of the kittens grew to be the size of the parents except Kitten 4. One of the kittens got less food than any of the others. Which of the kittens was it?

    A. Kitten 1

    B. Kitten 2

    C. Kitten 3

    D. Kitten 4

5. **Use Evidence** Describe the evidence that supports your answer to question 4.

_____

_____

6. **Explain** Which statement best explains why food could affect a kitten's size?

    A. Inherited traits tend to change in offspring.

    B. Inherited traits are exactly the same for all the siblings.

    C. Inherited traits can be influenced by the environment.

    D. Inherited traits among siblings do not get shared equally.

How can you use evidence to support that a (trait) is inherited?

Materials
• Nests Sheet

Science Practice

Scientists analyze data to provide evidence for phenomena.

Phenomenon Ecologists collect data from nature to analyze. How can you analyze the data to show that offspring inherit traits from their parents?

Write a Procedure

☐ **1.** Look at the Nests Sheet. What information can you observe about each type of bird?

_____

_____

☐ **2.** Choose one trait to investigate. How can you collect evidence about inheritance and variation of traits from the data on the Nests Sheet?

_____

_____

_____

_____

☐ **3.** Use the Nests Sheet to complete the table.

Trait studied: _____

Year	Turkey vulture	American robin	Grey partridge
1			
2			
3			
4			

Analyze and Interpret Data

4. Is the trait you investigated an inherited trait? Provide evidence to support your answer.

_____

_____

_____

_____

_____

5. Is there variation in the trait within a group of birds of the same kind? Provide evidence to support your answer.

_____

_____

_____

_____

_____

_____

_____

_____

_____

_____

Adaptations and Survival

Next Generation Science Standards

3-LS2-1 Construct an argument that some animals form groups that help members survive.

3-LS4-2 Use evidence to construct an explanation for how the variations in characteristics among individuals of the same species may provide advantages in surviving, finding mates, and reproducing.

3-LS4-3 Construct an argument with evidence that in a particular habitat some organisms can survive well, some survive less well, and some cannot survive at all.

3-LS4-4 Make a claim about the merit of a solution to a problem caused when the environment changes and the types of plants and animals that live there may change. .

Go online to access
your digital course.

VIDEO

eTEXT

INTERACTIVITY

VIRTUAL LAB

GAME

ASSESSMENT

The Essential Question

What happens to living things when their environments change?

Show What You Know

Look at the photo. Identify as many different living things as you can.

_____

_____

Quest Kickoff

STEM ▸ Help the Pond Organisms Survive

How can a construction project affect living things?

Phenomenon Hi, I'm Morgan Parker, a conservation biologist with a local environmental organization. In this problem-based learning activity, you will predict the effects of the planned construction project on a pond environment.

Some people are concerned that the project might affect living things in and near the pond. They have suggested solutions to protect the living things. As an expert, you will evaluate these solutions. Then, you will advise the community on how to reduce the possible effects of the construction on living things.

Follow the path to learn how you will complete the Quest. The Quest activities in the lessons will help you complete the Quest! Check off your progress on the path when you complete an activity with a . Go online for more Quest activities.

Quest Check-In Lab 1

Lesson 1

Find out how plants and animals survive in their environments. Use your knowledge to figure a way to reduce the effects of the construction project.

Next Generation Science Standards

3-LS4-4 Make a claim about the merit of a solution to a problem caused when the environment changes and the types of plants and animals that live there may change.

VIDEO

Watch a video about a conservation biologist.

Quest Check-In 3

Lesson 3

Apply what you know about changes to the environment. Predict how plants and animals will respond to these changes.

Quest Check-In 2

Lesson 2

Learn about different ways that animals work together in groups. Communicate the different ways that some animals use groups to help them survive.

Quest Findings

Complete the Quest! Use what you learn to help the community reduce the effects of the planned construction on the living things.

Quest Kickoff   213

What clues do beak shapes give about birds?

Scientists study how birds eat by looking at beak shape and types of food. How can you use models of beaks to help explain how birds eat?

Materials
- beak materials (tweezers, chopsticks, spoons, tongs, straw)
- bird food materials (beads of various sizes, small pieces of yarn, test tube with water)
- Bird Beak sheet

Procedure

☐ **1.** Look at the hummingbird, the cardinal, and the eagle on the Bird Beak sheet. What do their beaks look like? Choose two of the beaks to model.

☐ **2.** Try to pick up the different types of bird food with the model beaks. Record your observations.

Analyze and Interpret Data

3. **SEP Explain** Use your observations. What does the shape of a beak tell you about a bird?

_____

_____

_____

_____

_____

_____

_____

_____

Science Practice

Scientists use models to construct explanations.

Observations

Cause and Effect

Cause-and-effect relationships show how two events are related. Causes are reasons. Effects are results. Use these strategies to help you identify causes and effects when reading informational texts.

- Ask yourself questions, "What happened?" or "How did it change?" to identify an effect.
- Ask yourself, "Why?" to identify the cause.
- Look for clue words such as *because* and *so*. They can signal cause and effect.

Read the text to find out why certain birds can eat certain foods.

GAME

Practice what you learn with the Mini Games.

hummingbird

cardinal

eagle

Bird Beaks

The birds in the pictures have different beaks. The hummingbird feeds on the nectar deep inside the flower. Its beak is long and narrow, so it can reach the nectar inside the flower. A hummingbird cannot eat seeds because its beak is not strong. The cardinal's beak is short and strong, so it can open seeds. The eagle can tear apart fish because it has a sharp, curved beak. Neither the hummingbird nor the cardinal can eat fish.

☑ READING CHECK **Cause and Effect** In the text passage, draw an arrow from each of the four causes to its effect.

Survival of Individuals

ENGINEERING ⟩ Connection

Animals come in almost every color you can think of—neon green frogs, bright red fish, and sunny yellow goldfinches. Animals also have many different patterns, such as spots, stripes, or patches. These patterns can help animals blend into their environments. Animals can hide from predators or from the prey they hunt.

When engineers make zoo habitats, they try to mimic the natural habitats of animals that live there. This helps the animal meet its needs, just as the animal's wild habitat does.

📓 **Write About It** Study the frog and its habitat in the photo. If you were the engineer, what would you include in a zoo habitat for that frog?

uInvestigate Lab

How do sea lions stay warm in cold waters?

Scientists study how some animals, such as sea lions, can survive in cold environments. How can you use evidence to answer the question in the title?

Procedure

☐ **1.** Predict whether a layer of fat will help a sea lion survive in its cold environment.

_____

☐ **2. SEP Plan and Conduct an Investigation** Make a plan to test your prediction. Show your plan to your teacher before you start. Record your observations.

Materials
- petroleum jelly
- cup
- water
- ice
- spoon

 Wash your hands after the lab.

Science Practice

Scientists use evidence to explain how things work.

Observations

Analyze and Interpret Data

3. Use Evidence How does the sea lion survive in its cold environment? Use evidence to explain.

_____

_____

_____

How do living things adapt to survive?

Living things have adaptations to help them stay alive, or **survive**. An **adaptation** is a trait that helps an organism survive, find mates, or reproduce.

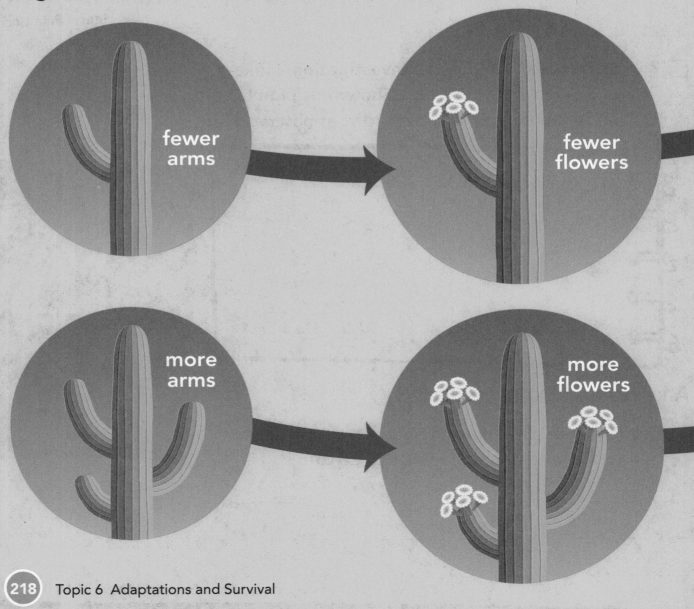

fewer arms

fewer flowers

more arms

more flowers

Individuals of the same kind may have different traits that provide advantages. A saguaro cactus with more arms can produce more offspring.

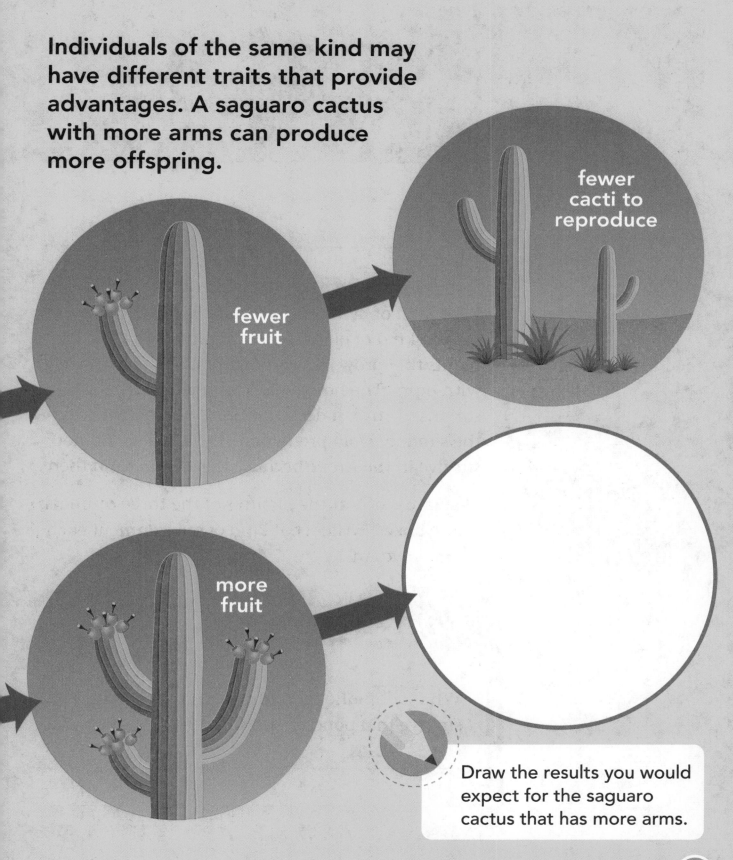

fewer fruit

fewer cacti to reproduce

more fruit

Draw the results you would expect for the saguaro cactus that has more arms.

Animal Needs for Survival

polar bear	tree frog	camel

Survival in Different Habitats

Each kind of living thing is adapted to live in a certain kind of place. For example, some kinds of plants that grow in cold parts of Earth are covered with hairs. The hairs help keep them warm. A sandfish lizard, a desert animal, digs holes in the sand to avoid predators. The lizard would not survive in the Arctic because there is no sand there.

Evaluate Look at the pictures of the three animals. In the boxes, write what kind of environment each animal lives in.

Quest Connection

What adaptations would an animal need to survive in a pond environment?

_____

_____

Differences Can Help Living Things

A species is a group of living things of the same kind. Each kind of animal and plant is a separate species. Individuals of the same species may have different traits, or adaptations, that help them survive and reproduce. An individual is more likely to have offspring when it has traits that make it better able to attract mates. Finding mates is one way a species can survive. For example, male widowbirds with longer tails attract more females for mating than male widowbirds with shorter tails.

INTERACTIVITY

Complete an activity about camouflage.

☑ Lesson 1 Check

1. **☑ READING CHECK Cause and Effect** Suppose a sea lion cannot eat enough food to keep its thick layer of fat. How might this change affect the sea lion?

_____

_____

_____

2. **Use Evidence** Galápagos tortoises survive by eating plants. Tortoises that live on islands with tall plants have long necks. Tortoises that live on islands with short plants have short necks. What conclusion can you draw from this evidence?

_____

_____

_____

How are living things suited to their habitats?

Materials
- string
- hand lens
- ruler
- craft sticks

Biologists study living things and their environments to understand how they survive. How do plants and animals of the same kind differ in the same environment?

⚠ Do not touch any animals.

⚠ Wash your hands when finished.

Procedure

☐ **1.** As a class, select 1 square meter of a habitat to observe outside. Choose one plant species and one animal species that you can observe there.

☐ **2.** Make a plan to observe different members of the plant and animal species. Use the materials.

☐ **3.** Show your plan to your teacher before you begin. Record your observations.

Science Practice

Scientists engage in arguments based on evidence to draw conclusions about scientific data.

Living Things	Similarities	Differences

Analyze and Interpret Data

4. Infer Based on your observations, which traits do you think are most important for the survival of living things in this environment? Explain why you think so.

_____

_____

_____

_____

_____

_____

5. SEP Engage in Argument from Evidence The planned construction project may cause the pond to dry up. Choose one pond plant and one pond animal. What traits do you think the plant and animal have that will help them survive if the pond dries up? Explain.

_____

_____

_____

_____

_____

_____

Lesson 2

Survival of Groups

I can...

List some animals that form groups to help them survive.

3-LS2-1

Literacy Skill
Cause and Effect

Vocabulary
migrate

Academic Vocabulary
advantage

▶ **VIDEO**

Watch a video about the survival of groups.

SPORTS ▸ **Connection**

It is a sunny day. You are standing by the side of the road waiting for a bicycle race to go by. You hear cheering. You see brightly colored shirts appear. Soon, a line of bike racers zooms past you! The racers all follow closely behind each other. They race like this because the bikers use energy to move the air in front of them out of the way. The air slows them down. By drafting, or riding closely behind each other, the racers can save their energy and go faster. At certain times of the year, you may see large flocks of birds flying in V-shaped patterns. They are drafting too! The lead bird makes the air easier for the other birds to fly in.

Evaluate Circle the cyclist you think is using the most energy.

uInvestigate Lab

How do some birds fly so far?

Scientists study how groups of animals help each other. Why do these birds often fly in a V shape?

Materials
- electric fan
- square sheet of paper
- safety goggles

⚠ Wear safety goggles.

⚠ Do not touch the fan while it is on.

Science Practice

Scientists *collect and use evidence* to make an argument.

Procedure

☐ **1.** Fold a sheet of paper in half so that it makes a V shape. Hold it straight in front of the fan your teacher provides. Is it easy or difficult to hold the paper straight? Record your observations

☐ **2.** Use your V-shaped paper and three or more V-shaped papers of other classmates. Place them in front of the fan in different ways. Record your observations of how easy or difficult it is to hold the papers straight.

Alone	In a Group

Analyze and Interpret Data

3. SEP Use Evidence Does your evidence support the claim that migrating in flocks helps geese survive? Explain.

_____

_____

Why do animals form groups?

Some animals form groups to survive in their environment. This allows them to share food, protect each other, and help take care of young ones.

Protect

There is safety in numbers for baboons. Some members of the group eat while the others look out for trouble.

Keep warm

Even the worst weather on the planet is no problem with a group effort. Emperor penguins share body heat and protect one another from the wind.

Capture prey

Some predators work together to help capture prey that is much larger than themselves.

Raise young

Elephants form herds, or groups. Most female elephants help raise and protect each other's young.

Draw another group of animals that you know that lives or works as a group.

Share work

Leafcutter ants work together to feed their colony.

Animal Groups

Animals must do many tasks to stay alive. They must find food and avoid predators. They must raise their young. Many animals do not have much time in the day to rest. In groups, animals can help each other with all of these tasks. Making a group can give animals an advantage. An **advantage** is anything that helps the animal.

Animals have many ways of living in groups. Orca whales may live in small family groups. Prairie dogs live in groups with many families. Caribou herds in Alaska can have hundreds of thousands of animals. Big or small, groups can make animal lives easier.

Hypothesize What are some reasons why forming a group might not be an advantage for animals?

_____

_____

Quest Connection

Do you think living in groups is an advantage or disadvantage for animals living near a pond? Explain your answer.

_____

_____

_____

_____

Some animals make groups to survive changes in their environment. When seasons change, many groups of animals move to a new place. They migrate to places that better meet their needs during that season. When animals **migrate**, they move to a different place. Canada geese migrate south together every fall. The geese reach their destination more easily by working together.

Explain How can these meerkats help one another?

_____

_____

☑ **Lesson 2 Check**

1. ☑READING CHECK **Cause and Effect** What causes some animals to migrate?

_____

_____

_____

2. **Identify** Why do some animals live in groups?

_____

_____

_____

Let's Get Together

The pond ecosystem is home to many different types of animals. Some of those animals live in groups. Choose a pond animal that lives in groups.

What is the advantage of living in a group for these animals?

_____

_____

_____

Do you think that forming a group can help your animal survive if the pond ecosystem changes? Explain your answer.

_____

_____

_____

How can a spider stay underwater all day long?

Phenomenon The diving bell spider spends most of its life underwater. It cannot breathe naturally underwater. At the surface, the spider traps an air bubble in the hairs on its back. It can use the air in the bubble to breathe. By staying underwater, the spider avoids land predators. It can also hunt prey that land spiders cannot hunt.

Now, put on your reasoning hat! What do you think would happen if one spider had more hair than another spider? Which would be better able to survive? Use evidence from the passage to write a science-based claim.

_____

_____

_____

_____

_____

_____

_____

Survival When Environments Change

STEM Connection

Think about your favorite animal or plant. Suppose that the animal or plant was no longer anywhere on Earth. How would you feel? Human actions can affect the survival of plants and animals. For example, many turtles are accidentally trapped in fishing nets. The turtles can die if they are not freed from the nets fast enough. Engineers have designed a device that prevents turtles from being tangled in the nets. It is called a Turtle Excluder Device, or TED for short. Using technology, engineers discover new ways to help save plants and animals from situations like this.

Construct What other solutions can you think of to save the turtles from being caught in dangerous fishing nets?

_____

_____

loggerhead turtle

How will sea levels affect *TIGERS*?

Conservation biologists study how changing environments affect specific kinds of animals. What will happen to tigers that live near the sea if ice in the regions around Earth's poles melts?

Materials
- cake pan
- 250 mL water
- 12 ice cubes
- ruler
- beaker
- safety goggles

Suggested Materials
- soil
- leaves
- sticks
- rocks
- spoon

Procedure

☐ **1.** Predict how a rising sea level might affect tigers that live near the sea.

_____

_____

☐ **2.** Design a model in the cake pan to investigate your prediction. Choose materials to model the land. Show your plan to your teacher before you begin.

☐ **3.** Add the water and ice. Measure the land from the end of the pan to the edge of the water. Record your data.

☐ **4.** Allow the ice to melt. Measure the amount of land to the edge of the water again.

⚠ Wear safety goggles.

Science Practice

Scientists use models to make arguments about cause and effect.

Analyze and Interpret Data

5. CCC Cause and Effect Use your data to explain how a rising sea level would affect the tigers living near the sea.

_____

_____

_____

_____

	How much land is there?
Before the ice melted	
After the ice melted	

Argue Using Evidence
Polar bears usually live in a habitat with cold temperatures. Discuss with a classmate how well a polar bear will survive if its environment becomes much warmer. Cite evidence for your argument.

Changes in the Environment

Living things depend on the environment to give them the things they need to survive. When the environment changes, plants and animals are affected too. Some changes are fast, such as when a wildfire kills plants. Other changes are slow and take many years to happen. For example, changes in climate over time can cause glaciers to melt and increase sea levels.

Changes in the environment are caused by humans, other organisms, and natural events. For example, humans cut down trees to build new homes or highways. Beavers cut down trees to build dams. Weather and climate changes can result in more or less rainfall. All of these changes affect landscapes, waterways, and the plants and animals living in the area.

Infer How might an increase in rainfall affect the plants and animals that live in an environment?

_____

_____

_____

Case Study: Denali National Park

Much of Denali National Park in Alaska is covered in glaciers. Earth's climate has become warmer over the years. One result is that there are fewer northern goshawks in the park. These birds feed on animals that do best in cold weather.

Another result is that glaciers now begin to melt much earlier in spring. Mosquitoes lay eggs in the puddles of melting ice. So, there are more mosquitoes now. The mosquitoes feed on caribou blood. More mosquitoes cause greater stress on the caribou. This has resulted in fewer caribou in the national park.

The increase in mosquitoes has an **impact**, or strong effect, on other animals too. Yellow-rumped warblers feed on mosquitoes. Because the warblers have more food, there are more of them now.

Write About It Denali National Park wants to decrease the number of mosquitoes in the park. In your science notebook, write how this change can affect the other animals in the park.

How do animals respond to SEASONAL CHANGES?

Animals have adaptations that help them survive when seasons change.

MIGRATION

Some butterflies **migrate**, or move to another location, when seasons change. Before winter, they may migrate to a warmer place, where they can find food. They return to their original locations during spring.

! Circle one reason butterflies migrate.

HIBERNATION

Bats **hibernate**, or stay in a state of rest, during winter when there is less food. When bats hibernate, they need less food. In spring, bats can find food easily.

! Underline the words that tell how hibernating helps bats survive.

MOLT

As seasons change, bison molt. When animals molt, they shed and then regrow their body covering. Bison grow thick fur to keep warm during winter. In spring, they shed their fur.

Plants Respond to Seasonal Changes

Like animals, plants have adaptations that help them survive seasonal changes in their environments.

The plant in the picture is a caladium. During the dry season, caladiums become **dormant**, or go into a state of rest. This adaptation helps protect the plant when less water is available in its environment. The roots of these caladiums store food and water to help the plant survive while it is dormant.

✓ READING CHECK Cause and Effect What causes caladiums to go dormant? How does that help the plants survive?

_____

_____

Quest Connection

▼ ▼

Suppose the construction project will take place during the winter months. How do you think the pond plants will respond as the top part of the pond freezes?

_____

_____

_____

Plants also respond to differences in temperature as the seasons change. Some flowering plants, such as these camellia bushes, lose their leaves when temperatures become colder. First, the plants stop making the substance they need to make food. Then, the leaves change color. Finally, the leaves fall from the plant. The leaves grow back in spring. Some trees, such as firs and pine trees, keep their leaves when temperatures become colder.

Infer Suppose a plant begins to grow leaves in spring. Then an unusual period of cold weather occurs. What do you think will happen to the plant?

_____

_____

_____

_____

_____

INTERACTIVITY

Complete an activity about the effects of environmental changes.

Plan It!

Freezing rain has covered the peach trees with ice. These trees do not have an adaptation that protects them from this type of weather. Ice can kill the flowers. How can you protect the trees from ice? Begin by listing three criteria, or desired features, of your solution.

_____

_____

_____

_____

Observe Changes

While on a walk or in your backyard, observe a specific plant for a few weeks. Record any changes you notice as the days go by. Has the plant changed in appearance? Has the environment changed? Draw conclusions about what you observe.

Changes in Environmental Conditions

Natural events and human activities can affect the environment. How do animals respond? Some animals move in and out of changing environments. For example, if a forest is cut down for new homes, resources that an animal needs may be lost. The animal may move to a similar environment where resources are available.

Plants cannot move like animals can. They may die if their environment changes too much. For example, if an area of land floods, the plants there may not survive.

✔ Lesson 3 Check

1. **Identify** What are different ways that animals might respond to a seasonal change such as a cold winter?

   _____

   _____

   _____

   _____

2. **Use Evidence from Text** Pick one plant or animal that lives in a forest. Think about how the plant or animal would respond to a forest fire. How does the organism's response help it survive? Use evidence to support your answer.

   _____

   _____

   _____

   _____

A Changing Pond Environment

The construction project is well under way. Construction workers have cut down trees to make room for buildings and have paved new roads. Bulldozers have flattened land. The stream will no longer flow to the pond. Soon the pond will dry up!

Predict How do you think the pond plants and animals will respond to these changes?

_____

_____

_____

_____

_____

uEngineer It! Design STEM

▶ **VIDEO**

Watch a video about designing outdoor recreation areas.

Have Your Fun, and Be Considerate Too!

Phenomenon People use outdoor parks and recreation areas as a place to have fun or to enjoy nature. This ski and snowboard park is in a natural environment. Skiers zip past snow-covered trees. The park is home to various plants and animals. Many parks are designed to protect the natural environment. The plants and animals that live there are an important part of the park.

Design It

Design a recreation area to fit the natural environment shown in
the picture. Make sure your recreation area protects the plants
and animals that live there. Draw your design on the picture. Label
the parts.

 How does your design protect the plants and animals that
live in the environment?

_____

_____

_____

INTERACTIVITY

Complete an activity to support your Quest findings.

STEM › **Help the Pond Organisms Survive**

How can a construction project affect living things?

Phenomenon Your community is concerned about how the construction project will affect the pond's plants and animals. They have proposed two solutions to reduce the impact of the change.

- Redirect another stream to flow to the pond.

- Fill the pond with water every month.

Make an Argument

Choose the proposed solution that you think will help the living things at the pond most. Or think of your own solution. Make an argument that explains why this solution is the most helpful. Cite evidence to support your argument. Present your argument to your classmates and teacher! You can make a presentation, write a report, or film a video.

Conservation Biologist

Conservation biologists work to protect natural resources, including land and living things. Their goal is to find ways to keep these systems healthy. They also help restore the health of unhealthy systems in nature.

Conservation biologists need a college degree, usually in biology, which is the study of living things. They must be able to talk with many kinds of people. Some work for companies or government agencies. Others might work as consultants. Consultants work with other people who hire them as needed. A conservation biologist might consult with farmers or other landowners. Some work to educate people about threats to ecosystems and what they can do about it.

📓 Make Meaning

In your science notebook, write about why you think conservation biologists are important.

1. **Cause and Effect** Choose the best explanation for why the frog is the same color as the plants in its habitat.

   A. The frogs are green because they want to look like each other.

   B. The frogs are green because they get their color from eating green plants.

   C. The frogs are green because they absorb the same sunlight that plants do.

   D. The frogs are green because matching their environment helps them survive.

2. **Use Evidence** Can forming a group help animals survive? Give two examples to support your claim.

   _____

   _____

   _____

   _____

3. **Vocabulary** Look at the picture of the birds flying. Use vocabulary learned in this lesson to describe what they are doing and why they are doing it.

   _____

   _____

   _____

   _____

4. **Systems** Most of the grove snails in a grassy area are yellow. In a nearby forest area, most of the grove snails are brown. Construct an explanation for why this is.

   _____

   _____

   _____

   _____

   _____

   _____

5. Vocabulary A new shopping center was being built near a neighborhood. The neighbors were upset that the woodpeckers left the area after the trees were cut down. Propose a solution to this problem and explain why it would work.

_____

_____

_____

_____

_____

_____

_____

_____

6. Vocabulary Use the term _dormant_ to describe how some plants respond when the seasons change.

_____

_____

_____

_____

7. Systems Which type of animal would you be most likely to find in a desert habitat?

A. an animal that survives well in hot, wet environments

B. an animal that survives well where water is hard to find

C. an animal that survives well where there are many trees

D. an animal that survives well in an area with tall mountains

The Essential Question _What happens to living things when their environment changes?_

Show What You Learned

Based on the evidence you studied, how do plants and animals respond when their environments change?

_____

_____

_____

_____

Read the paragraph about anole lizards and look at the table. Then answer the questions.

Anoles are lizards. Different kinds of anoles live on different kinds of plants. Anoles with shorter legs can walk on thin branches. Anoles with long legs cannot, but they are faster runners on the ground. Anoles eat different kinds of insects and smaller lizards. All anoles have a dewlap. A dewlap is a fan of skin under the lizard's chin. A brighter dewlap helps the anole attract a mate. Parents with a bright dewlap tend to have young with bright dewlaps also.

Anole Traits		
	Favorite branch size	**Eats**
green anoles	very thin	crickets, mealworms
brown anoles	thin	insects, green anoles
twig anoles	thick	spiders, flies
bark anoles	very thick	crickets, spiders

1. **Cause and Effect** Brown and twig anoles both live on the same island. Over time, the branches there get thicker. Make a prediction about what will happen to the numbers of brown and twig anoles over time. Explain why you made your prediction.

_____

_____

_____

_____

2. **Evaluate** Which type of anole lizard most likely has the shortest legs?

   A. green anoles

   B. brown anoles

   C. twig anoles

   D. bark anoles

3. **Use Evidence** Which piece of evidence supports your answer to question 2?

   A. Long legs are best for running fast.

   B. Long legs are best for thick branches.

   C. Short legs are best for thin branches.

   D. Short legs are best for catching crickets.

4. **Cause and Effect** A group of bark anoles was put on an island where no other anoles had been before. The first anoles had dewlaps that were very different. Over time, all of the offspring born on the island had brightly colored dewlaps. What caused this to happen?

   A. Anoles with bright dewlaps were better able to find food.

   B. Anoles with bright dewlaps were better able to find mates.

   C. Anoles with bright dewlaps were not as good at finding food.

   D. Anoles with bright dewlaps were not as good at finding mates.

How well will the rabbit *SURVIVE*?

Materials
- lamp
- white cloth
- black cloth
- thermometers

Suggested Materials
- small boxes

Phenomenon On a summer day, a pet black rabbit accidentally got loose in the Arizona desert. This rabbit is not native to the desert. The desert cottontail rabbit is native to the desert. The data table compares the characteristics of each kind of rabbit. Will the escaped rabbit survive in the desert?

⚠ Do not touch hot lamp.

Black rabbit	Desert cottontail
dark fur	light fur
floppy ears	upright ears
needs fresh water	gets water from food

Science Practice

Scientists use models to help to explain the world around them.

Procedure

☐ **1.** Write your hypothesis. How well could the black rabbit survive in the desert during the summer?

_____

_____

☐ **2.** Make a plan to test your hypothesis.

_____

_____

_____

_____

_____

_____

☐ **3.** Get your teacher's approval before you begin. Conduct your test. Record your data.

Analyze and Interpret Data

4. Evaluate Data Does the evidence support your hypothesis? Explain.

_____

_____

_____

_____

5. Use Evidence Construct an argument about the survival chances of the escaped rabbit in the summer. Use evidence to support your claim.

_____

_____

_____

_____

_____

Observations

6. Predict Which rabbit is most likely to be captured by a predator? Explain.

_____

_____

Fossil
Evidence

Next Generation Science Standards

3-LS4-1 Analyze and interpret data from fossils to provide evidence of the organisms and the environments in which they lived long ago.

3-LS4-3 Construct an argument with evidence that in a particular habitat some organisms can survive well, some survive less well, and some cannot survive at all.

▶ VIDEO

📖 eTEXT

👆 INTERACTIVITY

🧪 VIRTUAL LAB

🎮 GAME

☑ ASSESSMENT

The Essential Question

How have living things and environments changed?

Show What You Know

The fossil of an ancient whale was found in the Western Desert of Egypt. What does this fossil tell you about the environment of Egypt in the past?

_____

_____

Written in Stone

What can you find out from fossils?

Phenomenon Hello there! I am Tanya Hayden, paleontologist and fossil hunter. My team has collected fossils from different digs. Unfortunately, the labels got mixed up. I need your help to figure out where the fossils came from.

Like a paleontologist, you will look at each fossil. Then you will use what you know about fossils to decide where each one came from.

Follow this path to learn how you will complete the Quest. The Quest activities will help you complete the Quest successfully. Check off your progress on the path when you complete an activity with a QUEST CHECK ✓ OFF . Go online for more Quest activities.

Quest Check-In 1

Lesson 1

Gather clues from fossils.

Next Generation Science Standards
3-LS4-1 Analyze and interpret data from fossils to provide evidence of the organisms and the environments in which they lived long ago.

VIDEO

Watch a video about fossils.

Quest Check-In Lab 3

Lesson 3
Use what you have
learned to match
fossils to possible
source sites.

Quest Check-In 2

Lesson 2
Compare fossils to
similar organisms
that live today.

Quest Findings

Use the evidence you
collected to make
a hypothesis about
where fossils
come from.

What can a fossil tell you?

Scientists interpret data from fossils to find out about the organisms that formed them. What can you learn from a fossil?

Materials

- modeling clay

Suggested Materials

- leaf
- pine tree needles
- plastic insects
- shell
- pinecone

Procedure

☐ **1.** Choose one object. Write a plan to make a model of a fossil with it. Show your plan to your teacher before you begin.

☐ **2.** Exchange fossils with a classmate. Observe the fossils. Record your observations.

 ⚠ Wash your hands after the lab.

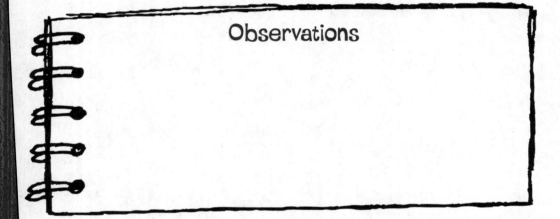

Observations

Science Practice

Scientists analyze and interpret data to answer questions.

Analyze and Interpret Data

3. **SEP Analyze and Interpret Data** What evidence does your classmate's fossil give you about the "living thing" that made it? Analyze data you collected.

_____

_____

_____

_____

_____

Use Evidence from Text

Evidence is a clue that can be observed. It helps you explain things. You can collect clues and use the information to form new ideas. Here is how to use evidence from text:

- Find the main idea of the text.
- Underline or circle specific facts.
- Ask if the facts support the main idea.

Read this paragraph. Look for evidence from the text.

🎮 GAME

Practice what you learn with the Mini Games.

A Wall of Bones

Dinosaur National Monument, Utah, has a rocky pit with more than 1,500 dinosaur bones. Visitors can touch dinosaur bones exactly where a river dropped them nearly 150 million years ago. Scientists chipped away some of the rock, leaving the bones in the stone. They uncovered bones from more than 400 individual dinosaurs, including allosaurs, diplodocuses, and stegosauruses. These bones make up a wall almost 46 meters long. This wall is a one-of-a-kind display.

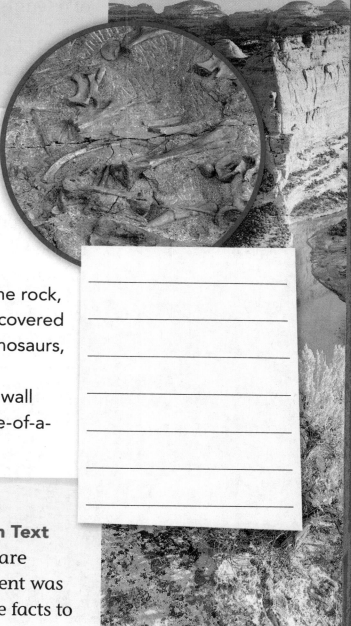

☑ **READING CHECK** **Use Evidence from Text**
Underline three facts in the passage that are evidence that Dinosaur National Monument was home to many dinosaurs. Use one of these facts to write a caption for this photo.

Fossils

I can...
Describe what a fossil is.
Describe some ways that fossils form.
3-LS4-1

Literacy Skill
Use Evidence from Text

Vocabulary
fossil
extinct

Academic Vocabulary
evidence

 VIDEO

Watch a video about how fossils form.

SPORTS ⟩ **Connection**

Making a tennis ball begins with sheets of a rubber and clay mixture. The sheets are placed on a mold. The top part of the mold presses the latex into the bottom part. This makes one half of a tennis ball.

Similar to a tennis ball, when the body of a dead organism presses into the ground below it, it leaves a print. Sometimes the print stays empty like a tennis ball. Other times, the print is filled in by other materials. These materials take the shape of the print. The empty print and the filled in print are different types of fossils. Not all fossils form like a tennis ball. Some are formed when the organism's body stays but minerals stick to it and make it hard like a rock.

☑ **READING CHECK** **Use Evidence from Text**
Underline three steps for making a tennis ball.

uInvestigate Lab

How do minerals help form fossils ?

Scientists sometimes find fossils that look like hard bone. How can you model what happens when minerals stick to a bone?

Materials
• safety goggles
• plastic gloves
• sponge
• salt
• warm water
• clear cup
• spoon

Suggested Materials
• saucer

Procedure

☐ **1.** Make a plan to investigate how minerals could fossilize tissue without changing their shape. Use the materials for your plan.

_____

_____

_____

_____

⚠ Wear safety goggles.

⚠ Wear plastic gloves.

☐ **2.** Show your plan to your teacher before you begin.

Analyze and Interpret Data

3. SEP Explain What does each part of your model represent? How does this model represent what happens to some fossils?

_____

_____

_____

Science Practice

Scientists use models to study natural processes.

4. Infer What are some reasons that this process may not happen to all fossils?

_____

_____

_____

Literacy ▸ Toolbox

Use Evidence from Text
Evidence is based on observations. Suppose you were told by a friend that fossils can form anywhere. Would you agree? Find evidence in the text to support your answer.

Kinds of Fossils

You might think that the photo shows a plant that is living today. But this plant lived millions of years ago. What you see is a fossil that formed from the ancient plant. **Fossils** are the remains of living things or traces of living things that lived very long ago. A trace is a footprint, burrow, or other mark left by a living thing.

Scientists have found fossils that are billions of years old! A fossil can be so small that you cannot see it with just your eyes. Or it can be as large as a dinosaur. Fossils of a whole organism are rare. Most fossils form from the hard parts of living things, such as bones, shells, and teeth.

Most organisms do not form fossils. They decay or are eaten after they die. Fossils only form in certain conditions. One important condition is that the body or trace of an organism must be quickly buried by mud, sand, or other materials. This most often happens on the bottom of rivers, swamps, lakes, or oceans.

Draw Conclusions Draw a kind of animal mark that might become a fossil.

Fossil Evidence

One reason that scientists study fossils is to gather evidence about different organisms and their environments. **Evidence** is information that supports that something is true. For example, fossil footprints are evidence that an animal walked in the place where the fossil was found. That information tells scientists that the area was not covered with water when the animal was alive. The footprints in the photo were made when a dinosaur walked through mud. The mud dried. Over a very long time, the mud became rock. The footprint became a trace fossil. Animal burrows, nests, eggshells, and dung can also become trace fossils. Each one gives different information about the animal and the time in which the animal lived. For example, dung fossils provide evidence of what some animals ate.

Write About It Suppose that 50 million years from now, a scientist uncovers your room in a fossil dig. In your science notebook, describe what trace fossils of your past activities the scientist might find.

uBe a Scientist

Make a Fossil
Make your own trace fossil. In a pan, mix together water and earth from your neighborhood. Press your handprint into the mud and carefully remove your hand. Let this dry. What information does this fossil give about you?

Quest Connection

What can fossils of footprints tell us about the animals that made them?

_____

_____

_____

Visual Literacy Connection

How does a fossil form?

1
2
3
A fish dies in the ocean. Its body sinks to the ocean floor.
The fish's body is quickly covered with layers of mud or sand on the ocean floor.
Water flows through the rock and dissolves the remains of the fish. The empty space left behind is a fossil mold.

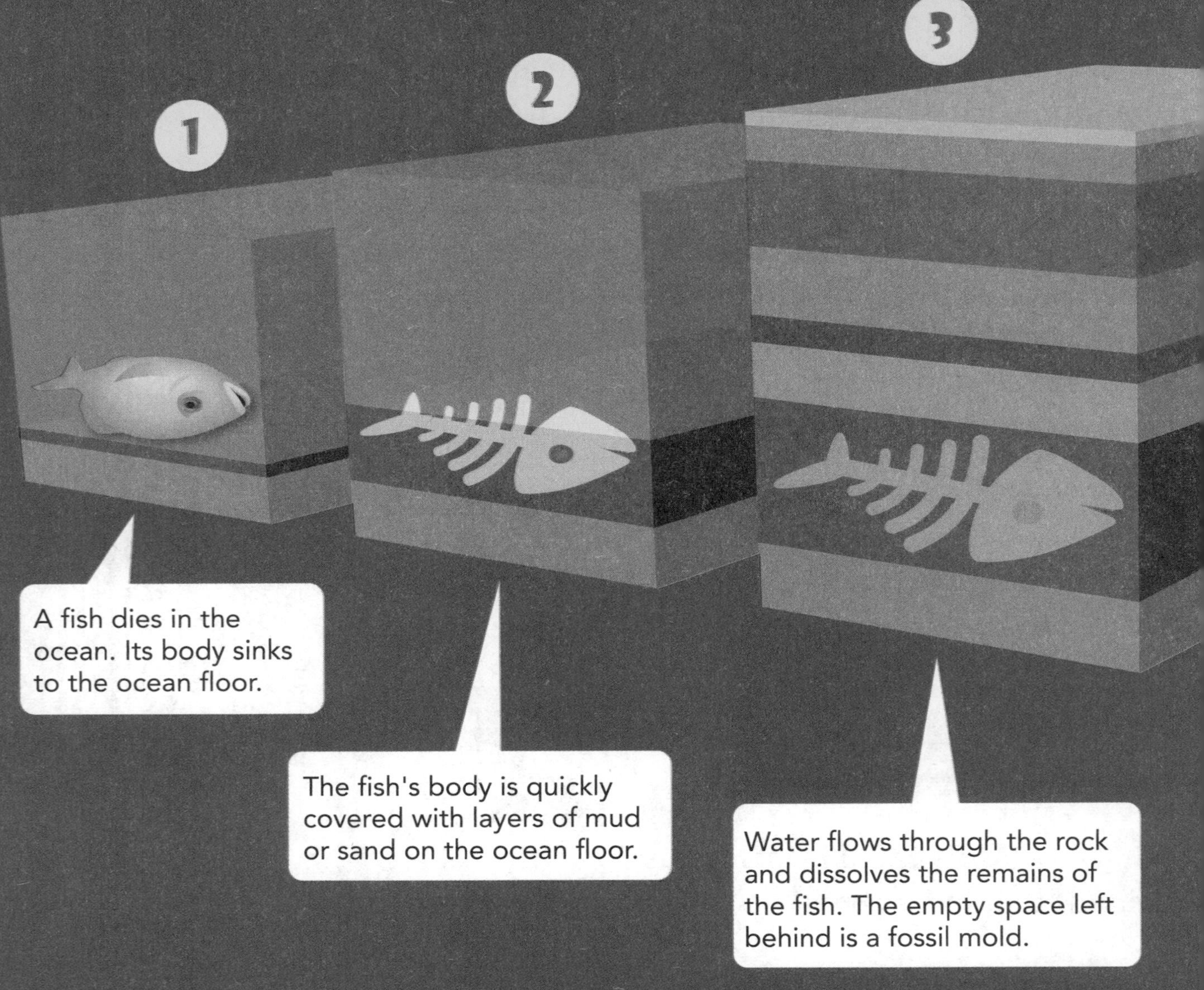

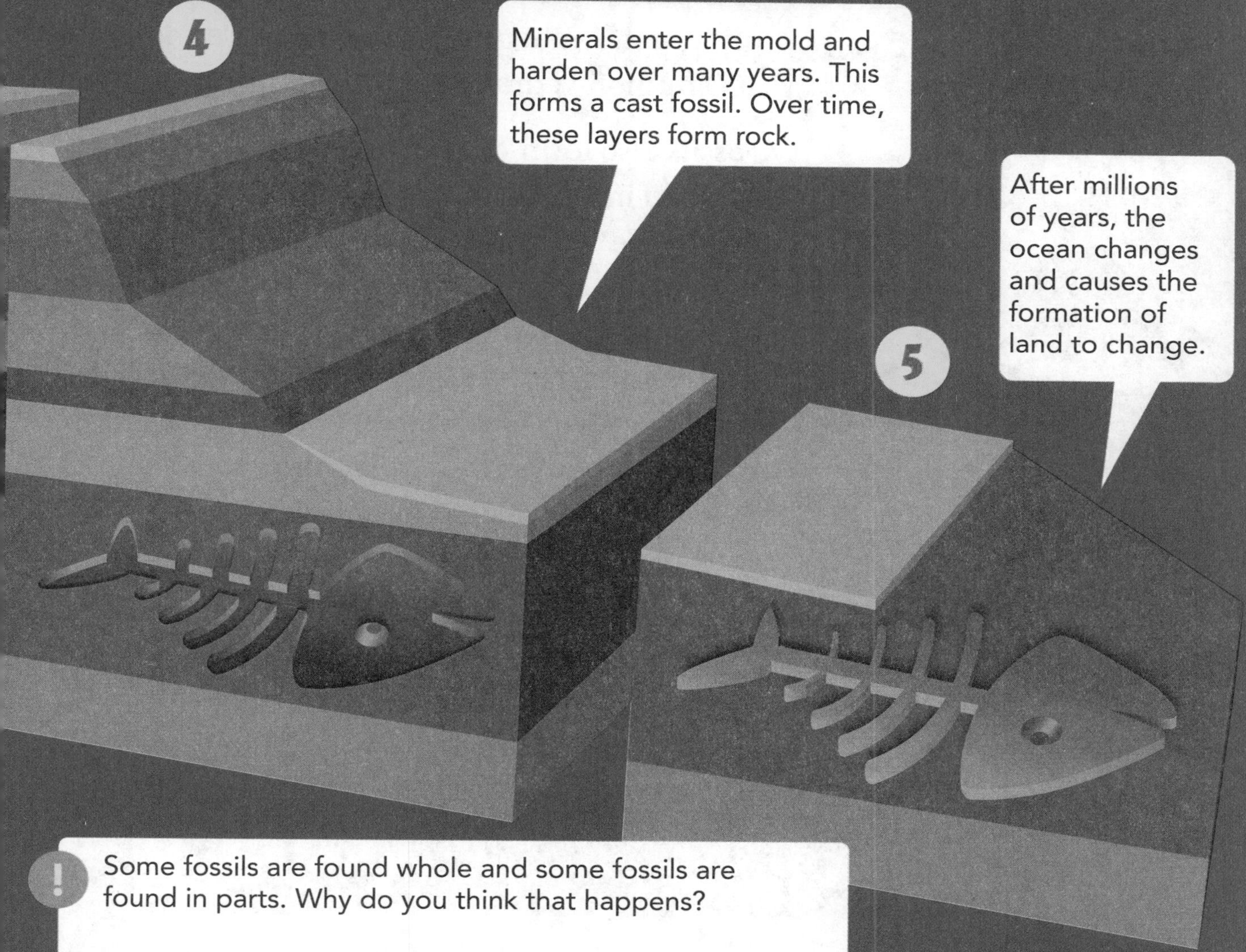

4

Minerals enter the mold and harden over many years. This forms a cast fossil. Over time, these layers form rock.

After millions of years, the ocean changes and causes the formation of land to change.

5

Some fossils are found whole and some fossils are found in parts. Why do you think that happens?

_____

_____

_____

Fossils in Sap and Ice

Not all fossils are found in rock. Some fossils are in ancient tree resin. These fossils form when resin oozes down a tree trunk. The resin can trap small animals, such as insects, or small plants. The resin hardens over time and forms honey-colored amber. You can see in the photo how well amber preserves the body of an insect. Amber fossils can be more than 100 million years old.

Fossils also form when living things become trapped in ice. Woolly mammoths, like the one in the picture, lived across many parts of Earth until about 4,000 years ago. Scientists have found several frozen mammoths. The mammoths froze when the climate was colder than it is today. Because they were frozen, many of the soft body parts of the mammoths did not decay. Scientists can gather different kinds of information from soft body parts than from hard parts such as bone. Some of the information helps them figure out how the animal moved, what it ate, and what its body shape was.

Question It!

A paleontologist discovers a fossil in ice. It is the remains of an unusual fish. The paleontologist has never seen this kind of fish before. Write two questions that the paleontologist might ask to find out how it formed.

_____

_____

_____

Fossils in Tar

Another kind of fossil formed in tar pits. Tar pits are areas filled with a sticky material that seeps to Earth's surface from inside Earth. An example is the La Brea tar pits in California. Thousands of years ago, animals there became trapped in the tar. Most of the animals were meat eaters. Scientists think that groups of animals chased prey into the tar pit. Both the prey and meat-eating animals became trapped. The tar preserved their skeletons.

Many of the kinds of organisms that formed fossils are **extinct**, or no longer live on Earth. Dinosaurs are an extinct kind of animal. Today we find the fossilized bones of dinosaurs. Scientists have learned a lot by studying the fossils.

Draw Conclusions What do you think scientists can learn by studying a fossil bone of a dinosaur?

:_____

_____

▶ INTERACTIVITY

Complete an activity about exploring fossils.

☑ Lesson 1 Check

1. **Describe** What is a fossil?

   _____

   _____

2. **Explain** Two ancient plants died at the same time. One was near a river; the other was on a grassy hillside. Which would be more likely to become a fossil? Explain why.

   _____

   _____

Plant, Animal, or Trace

To begin your Quest, you will start gathering information about the three fossils in the photos.

For each photo, tell whether it is a plant fossil, an animal fossil, or a trace fossil. Also write what else you can observe about the fossil.

1. Fossil: plant, animal, trace

_____

_____

_____

_____

2. Fossil: plant, animal, trace

_____

_____

_____

_____

3. Fossil: plant, animal, trace

_____

_____

_____

_____

Measure

Scientists make careful, exact measurements. The metric ruler shows that this fossil, called a trilobite, is 9 centimeters long. Use a metric ruler to measure the different parts of this fossil reptile. Always measure twice to make sure you have the right measurements.

Body part	Length
whole body (head to tip of tail)	
head	
left shoulder to elbow	
tail	
back right foot	

Fossils as a Record

I can...

Use fossil data to give evidence of organisms and environments that existed long ago.

3-LS4-1

Literacy Skill
Use Evidence from Text

Vocabulary
fossil record

Academic Vocabulary
data

▶ **VIDEO**

Watch a video about the geologic time scale.

STEM Connection

Paleontologists are going high-tech to study fossils in hard-to-reach places. Death Valley National Park in California has a canyon that has one of the largest and best-preserved groups of animal fossils. Only a few people are allowed into the canyon each year, so scientists use GPS satellites and specialized cameras to study the fossils they cannot visit in person. Photos have recorded fossil tracks left by mastodons, camels, tiny birds, and other animals that lived 5 million years ago. Scientists and park rangers try to protect such sites from visitors. In some places with fossils, people have stolen fossils for souvenirs.

📔 **Make Meaning** Do you think studying fossils is important? In your science notebook, explain your opinion.

uInvestigate Lab

What can fossil footprints tell you about an animal?

Trace fossils can give information that fossils of bones and other body parts cannot. What can you learn about an animal from its fossil footprint?

Materials
- Fossil Footprints sheet

Suggested Materials
- meterstick
- markers

Procedure

☐ **1.** Use the Fossil Footprints sheet to gather data about animals from millions of years ago. Use any of the materials to help you collect data.

☐ **2.** Record your observations.

Science Practice

Scientists analyze data to provide evidence.

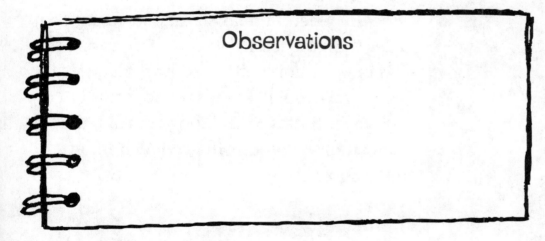

Observations

Analyze and Interpret Data

3. SEP Analyze What can you infer from the data you collected? What evidence did you use to make your inference?

_____

_____

_____

_____

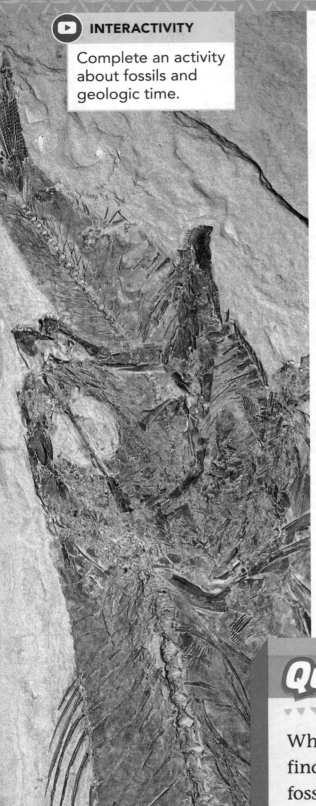

▶ **INTERACTIVITY**

Complete an activity about fossils and geologic time.

Clues from Fossils

Paleontologists gather **data**, or facts, from fossils. They might find a fossil of a sea animal in an area that is far from an ocean. That clue provides evidence that the area where the fossil organism was found was covered by an ocean in the past. Scientists can put together information for many fossils to figure out what an area was like when the fossils formed.

The age of a fossil is an important piece of data. One clue about the age of a fossil is the rock in which it is found. Rocks with fossils formed in layers over a very long time. Scientists have studied these layers. They know that each layer of rock formed at a different time. In general the fossils at a lower layer are older than the fossils above it. Scientists use this information to figure out when a fossil organism lived. If scientists find a fossil in a rock layer that is 65 million years old, they know that the organism lived 65 million years ago.

Quest Connection

What clues might a paleontologist look for to find out what the area was like at the time a fossilized organism lived?

_____

_____

_____

_____

_____

_____

The Fossil Record

Scientists use the information they gather from rocks and fossils to infer what Earth was like throughout its history. Scientists know that a record of Earth's past is found in the layers of rock and the fossils within them. Scientists can look at these fossils and find patterns. They have created a **fossil record** that includes the total number of fossils found. This fossil record gives clues about how organisms have changed over time. Scientists have used information from the fossil record to organize Earth's history into units of time.

Draw Conclusions How would organizing fossil evidence into a time scale help people learn about Earth's history?

_____

_____

Science Practice ▸Toolbox

Analyze and Interpret Data Scientists gather information. Then they analyze and interpret the information. They infer what it means. A team of paleontologists find a fossil at the bottom of a canyon. What does this location tell about the fossil?

When did animals appear on Earth?

Earth formed about 4.5 billion years ago. Scientists measure geologic time in eras. Follow the numbered sequence of eras. Read each era diagram from the bottom layer to the top layer to learn when different types of animals and plants appeared on Earth or became extinct.

1 Paleozoic

542 to 251 million years ago

3. A mass extinction took place about 252 million years ago. Most land animals and plants died.

REPTILES

Draw a fish fossil in the circle.

AMPHIBIANS

JAWED FISH

JAWLESS FISH

INVERTEBRATES

1. Early animals of this era lived in the ocean.

2. Early fish did not have jaws. Fish developed jaws later.

❸ Cenozoic

65.5 million years ago to today

Draw a monkey or ape fossil in the circle.

MODERN MAMMALS

MONKEYS AND APES

Monkeys and apes appeared between early mammals and today's mammals.

❷ Mesozoic

251 to 65.5 million years ago

2. Another extinction happened 65 million years ago. More than 70% of land animals and many plants became extinct.

DINOSAURS

Draw a dinosaur fossil in the circle.

1. Dinosaurs roamed the land, the seas, and the sky.

ARCHAEOPTERYX
A bird-like dinosaur

Index Fossils

The rock layer in which fossils are found is not the only clue to the age of the fossil organism. Scientists can also use other fossils from the same layer. Index fossils are fossils of organisms that lived for a short, known time. Index fossils must be plentiful at that time. They must also be easy to identify. The trilobite in the photo is an index fossil.

☑ Lesson 2 Check

1. **Infer** A new fossil is found. It is very similar to a type of fish that lives today. What can you infer about the environment of the fossil organism?

_____

_____

2. **Cite Evidence** What evidence do scientists use to organize the fossil record?

_____

_____

Long Ago and Today

You have taken notes about things you can observe in fossils.
Now compare the fossils to similar organisms that live today.
Write what you can infer about the fossil organisms from the
living organisms.

_____

_____

_____

_____

_____

_____

_____

_____

_____

_____

_____

_____

✑Engineer It! Model STEM

▶ **VIDEO**

Watch a video about how scientists use x-rays to study fossils.

Rebuilding Dinosaurs

Phenomenon Everyone would like to see what the body of a fossil organism really looked like. It is rare to find a fossil that shows a whole body. Only a few bones or trace fossils might be found. Even with a complete fossil, many characteristics of the fossil organisms will not be known. For example, we know a lot about dinosaurs. But fossils do not give clues to what color most kinds of dinosaurs were.

How could you build a model from the smaller fossilized parts of an organism? Computer engineers can help. They write programs that can infer 3-D models from incomplete fossils. They use computer-aided design, or CAD. The CAD program produces a possible model of what an organism looked like. Then a 3-D printer makes the model in layers of plastic.

Model It!

A realistic model of a dinosaur shows the organism's height, length, and shape. It also shows details, such as whether it had claws, toes, or eyes.

Suppose you are a paleontologist. You need to make a model to show how a fossil animal looked before it died. Your model can only be made from materials in your classroom.

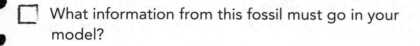

☐ What information from this fossil must go in your model?

☐ What must you infer to make your model?

☐ Draw your idea for your model. Label the materials that will be used to make each part.

☐ Show your drawing to your teacher. Then make your model!

Living Things and Climate Change

SPORTS Connection

Hockey and snowboarding are sports that people enjoy in the ice and snow. Baseball is not. In the past, most sports were played outside. Hockey took place in winter on frozen ponds. Golfers played on the green spring grass. People played baseball on warm, dry summer days.

Today, technology has changed how seasons affect sports. Indoor arenas make ice-skating possible all year. Machines make snow for skiers when winter weather does not. Even football has moved to indoor stadiums to avoid unpleasant weather. Even so, not all sports can avoid the weather. Baseball players in outdoor stadiums still stop playing when rain falls heavily.

Identify Underline facts that tell why weather no longer controls some sports.

uInvestigate Lab

How can you use evidence to infer climate change?

Scientists use fossil clues to tell what the climate of an area was long ago. How can you use fossils to recognize climate change?

Materials
• 4 colors of modeling clay
• plastic cup
• craft sticks
• Fossils sheet

Procedure

☐ **1.** Cut out the "fossils" on the Fossils sheet. Arrange them into three different climates.

☐ **2.** Use the materials to make a model of three layers of rock from a particular place. In each layer, insert a "fossil" from one of the three climates. Record the climate you modeled in each layer.

_____

_____

☐ **3.** Trade cups with another group. Dig for fossils in the model. Record what you discover.

_____

_____

Science Practice

Scientists use evidence to analyze and interpret data.

Analyze and Interpret Data

4. SEP Use Evidence What can you infer about the climate in the area during the period the rock layers formed? Cite evidence to support your claim.

_____

_____

_____

Changes over Time

From fossil clues, scientists know that the environments of a particular area have changed a lot over time. More than 250 million years ago, the Mojave Desert was covered by a shallow sea. Some of the organisms that lived there were very different from the organisms that live there today.

Then, between 225 and 65 million years ago, the seas dried up. The climate became dry and windy. Most organisms that had lived in the sea environment could not live in such a dry place. Desert plants, such as cacti and yucca, grew. Plants provided food for animals.

Circle animals that still live on Earth today.

Draw Conclusions Why do some animals and plants survive in the desert while others do not?

_____

_____

▶ **INTERACTIVITY**

Complete an activity about piecing together the past.

Insects and reptiles developed before mammals. Circle the lizards and snake in this ecosystem.

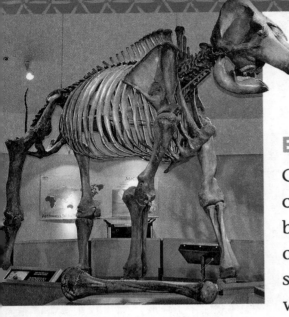

Ice Age mastodon fossils have been found in Florida.

Evidence of Climate Change

Climate on Earth has a pattern of warming and cooling. Scientists know that climate changes because they have fossil evidence. Different kinds of organisms need different climate conditions to survive. Some kinds of organisms cannot survive when even a small climate change happens.

Fossils of plant seeds give scientists good evidence for climate change. Different kinds of plants survive in different climates. If a seed of a particular kind of plant is found in a rock layer, scientists can infer what the climate was like when the plant was living.

Write About It In your science notebook, write a paragraph that tells what would happen to the living things in your town if the climate became much colder.

Quest Connection

How can you use fossil evidence to infer the kind of climate a fossil organism lived in?

_____

_____

_____

_____

Climate Change and Extinction

Scientists **argue**, or make claims supported by evidence. They use fossil evidence to argue that climate change can cause extinction. After big climate changes, some organisms no longer appear in the later fossil record. The kinds of organisms that could not live in the changed environment became extinct.

Scientists found this fossil of an extinct crocodile in a desert in Wyoming. In ancient times, a huge lake covered the area.

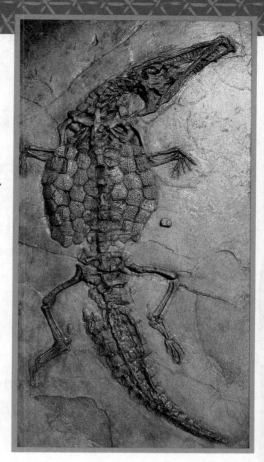

☑ READING CHECK **Use Evidence from Text**
Circle the evidence that explains why the crocodile became extinct.

☑ **Lesson 3 Check**

1. **Cite Evidence** What fossil evidence supports the claim that some organisms cannot survive climate change?

_____

_____

_____

2. **Construct an Argument** What evidence might show that some organisms survive climate change and others do not?

_____

_____

_____

_____

_____

Where did those fossils come from?

You have gathered information about three fossils. It is time to see whether you can use the information to match each fossil to the dig site it came from.

Materials
- Paleontologist Letter

Science Practice

Scientists *use evidence* to make arguments about the past.

Procedure

☐ **1.** Write the information you have gathered about each fossil in the Check-Ins for other lessons.

_____

_____

_____

_____

_____

_____

_____

☐ **2.** Read the letter from the paleontologist. Decide how to use the table to organize the information in the letter and information from the Check-Ins. Write the information in the table.

☐ **3.** **SEP Engage in Argument From Evidence** Use the information to determine which dig site each fossil most likely came from. Write the dig site in the table.

Stone around fossil	mudstone	shale stone	sandstone
Age of fossil	23 million years	300 million years	270 million years

Analyze and Interpret Data

4. **Compare and Contrast** Compare the dig sites you identified with those of classmates. Choose one of the fossils and record how other classmates used different methods to identify the dig site.

_____

_____

_____

_____

Written in Stone

What can you find out from fossils?

INTERACTIVITY

Organize data to support your Quest Findings.

Organize the Evidence

Phenomenon By now you should have decided where each of the fossils came from. You should also have identified the evidence you used to make the identification. Use that information to write a letter to Tanya Hayden, the paleontologist who asked for your help.

In your letter, tell her at which dig site you think each fossil was found. Include the process you went through to make your decision. Also include the evidence you used to match each fossil to the correct fossil dig.

QUEST CHECK ✓ **OFF**

Paleontologist

Paleontology is dirty work! Paleontology is the science of learning about past life on Earth through fossils. Paleontologists dig in dirt and rock to find fossils. They use brushes to remove dirt so the fossils are not broken. A single large fossil, such as a leg bone, may take weeks of digging and brushing. Then it is time to study the fossil. Study may be done at the dig site or in a lab.

Paleontologists must learn about Earth processes, living things, and the history of rocks on Earth. Paleontologists also study how to find, remove, and identify fossils. They use computers to help model fossils and the ancient Earth. Paleontologists need advanced college degrees. They make terrific, interesting teachers! Many teach college classes to share what they have learned.

📓 **Reflect** In your science notebook, explain why you might like to be a paleontologist.

1. **Interpret Diagrams** Eva has found two cliffs with nearly the same fossils. She needs help dating the different rock layers.

Sample 1 Sample 2

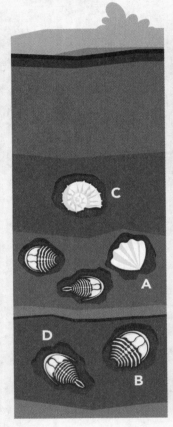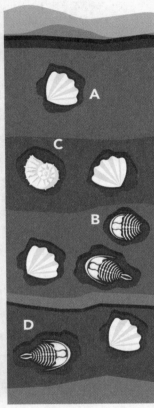

Which of these is an index fossil from the two rock samples?

A. fossil A

B. fossil B

C. fossil C

D. fossil D

2. **Vocabulary** Several fossils of a kind of lizard have been found. The lizard is extinct. What does this mean?

A. Lizards of this kind may be found somewhere else.

B. No more lizards live on Earth.

C. The lizard is thought to be an endangered species.

D. No more lizards of this kind live on Earth.

3. **Identify** What are two examples of trace fossils?

_____

_____

4. **Explain** Which statement shows fossil evidence of climate change?

A. A fossil of a wolf is found in a forest.

B. A fossil of a hippo is found in a riverbed.

C. A fossil of a shark is found in a desert.

D. A fossil of grass is found in a prairie.

5. Describe How do fossils show that some animals adjusted to the climate change and others did not?

_____

_____

_____

_____

_____

_____

_____

_____

_____

_____

6. Explain How can you tell how old a fossil is?

_____

_____

_____

_____

7. Interpret What evidence can you get from this photo of the fossil?

A. the color of the original fish

B. the type of scales on its skin

C. the time when the fish lived

D. the way that the fish moved

The Essential Question _How have living things and environments changed?_

Show What You Learned

You know what fossils tell us about the past. Use this knowledge to answer the Essential Question.

_____

_____

_____

_____

_____

_____

Look at the diagram of the fossil bed, and then answer
questions 1–4.

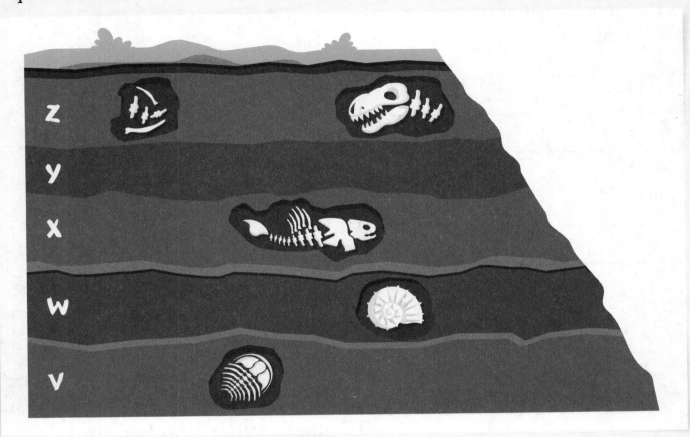

1. **Observe Patterns** Describe how the environment changed
   in this location.

   _____

   _____

2. **Use Evidence** Describe the evidence that supports your
   answer to question 1.

   _____

   _____

   _____

3. **Analyze Data** Which statement can be supported by the data in the diagram?

   A. All of the animals that left fossils have gone extinct.

   B. The animals in the top layer appeared on Earth first.

   C. All of the sea fossils formed at about the same time.

   D. The animals in the bottom layer were the first to live in this place.

4. **Apply Concepts** What might explain why no fossils are in layer Y?

   _____

   _____

5. **Interpret Data** In which layer would you expect to find a fossil of a tree?

   A. layer V

   B. layer W

   C. layer X

   D. layer Y

   E. layer Z

What were this organism and its environment like?

Science Practice

Scientists analyze and interpret data to answer questions.

Phenomenon Paleontologists use living organisms to draw conclusions about fossil organisms. What can you learn about a pterodactyl and its environment from a fossil?

Procedure

☐ **1.** Think about how animals survive in their environment. How can you use their features to determine where they live?

_____

_____

☐ **2.** Examine the photo of a fossil of an animal known as a pterodactyl. This kind of animal no longer lives on Earth.

☐ **3.** Describe some of the pterodactyl's features that you observed.

_____

_____

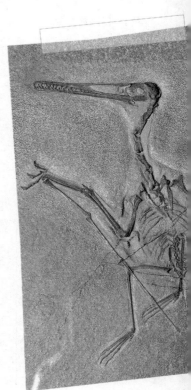

Analyze and Interpret Data

4. **Infer** What kind of food do you think a pterodactyl ate? Why?

_____

_____

_____

5. Explain How do you think the pterodactyl used its feet? Why?

_____

_____

_____

6. Compare Based on the bones of the fossil, what animal living today do you think the pterodactyl is most like?

_____

7. Infer Use the animal you identified and the fossil bones to draw what you think the pterodactyl might have looked like.

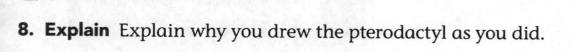

8. Explain Explain why you drew the pterodactyl as you did.

_____

_____

_____

Science Practices

Ask Questions

Science is the study of the natural world using scientific tools and methods. The natural world includes things such as matter, energy, the planets, and living things. It does not include things such as opinions about art or music.

A scientist asks questions and then tries to answer them. For example, a scientist might wonder how a large whale finds its food deep in the ocean. The scientist could first study what others have already learned. Then the scientist could investigate questions that have not been answered. Questions could include "How can a whale hold its breath underwater when it makes a deep dive?" Or, "How does a whale find food in the darkness of the deep ocean?"

Ask Questions What question would you ask about the animal in the photograph?

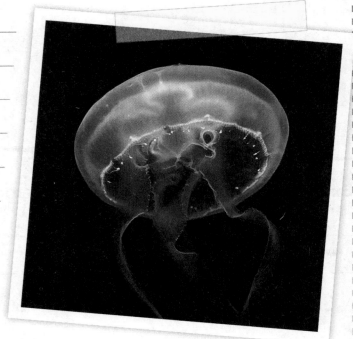

_____

_____

_____

_____

_____

_____

_____

SEP.1 Asking questions and defining problems
SEP.3 Planning and carrying out investigations
SEP.4 Analyzing and interpreting data

Carry Out Investigations

Scientists use investigations and experiments to do their work. Part of an investigation is to observe the natural world to learn about how it works. When scientists make observations, they do not change anything. Scientists collect data from their observations.

Quantitative data are expressed as numbers. Qualitative data describe something, such as how it smells or what color it is.

Scientists also investigate the world using experiments. In an experiment, scientists make a change to the object or process they are observing. For example, the amount of salt dissolved in ocean water is not the same everywhere. To find out how quickly salt dissolves in water at different temperatures, a scientist might put identical amounts of salt and water in several containers at different temperatures. The scientist changes the temperature of the containers and measures the time the salt takes to dissolve in each. The part of the experiment that the scientist changes is called the independent variable. The part that changes as a result is called the dependent variable. In this case, the independent variable is temperature, and the dependent variable is the time the salt takes to dissolve. All scientific investigations include collecting data.

Plan an Investigation A scientist is investigating how the amount of salt in water affects the growth of young fish. What are some quantitative data that the scientist can record?

_____

_____

_____

Science Practices

Science Tools

Scientists use tools to take measurements when they collect data. They also use tools to help make observations about the natural world. Scientific tools expand the type of observations that can be made.

Tools for measuring include rulers to measure length, certain glassware to measure volume, thermometers to measure temperature, and balances to measure mass. Different types of tools are needed for taking very small or very large measurements. It is important to use the right tool for the measurement that is to be taken.

Tools that expand what we can detect and measure include microscopes and telescopes. These tools allow people to observe things that are too small or too far away to see.

Cause and Effect Red tides occur when the population of tiny algae grows. The organisms can make toxic substances that harm wildlife and make the water unsafe for people. How would scientists use a microscope when they study a red tide?

_____

_____

_____

Digital Tools

Many modern tools operate using microprocessors or computers. These objects are digital tools. Digital tools include measuring tools such as digital balances and thermometers. They also include tools that scientists use to record and analyze data. Many scientific instruments have a computer that guides data collection and records results. Digital cameras are often a key part of telescopes, microscopes, and other tools used to make observations.

A solar panel provides power for the digital instruments and computer on this buoy. The instruments can measure changes in the ocean.

Computers and other digital devices make data collection faster. Processors can respond to changes and record data much faster than a human observer can. Computers are also important for keeping records and analyzing large numbers of data. Computers and other digital devices are an important part of communication networks that allow scientists to share data and results.

Communicate Scientists communicate in different ways. How could a scientist use a computer to communicate with another scientist?

_____

_____

Science Practices

Analyzing and Interpreting Data

Scientists use empirical evidence when they study nature. Empirical evidence is information that can be observed and measured. Scientific conclusions are always based on evidence that can be tested. These observations and measurements are data that can be used to explain the natural world.

Measurements and observations provide scientists with evidence of changes. For example, when a natural system changes, the change can affect organisms in the system. Scientists can observe and record the changes, such as how many organisms are living in an area at one time compared to another time. Then the scientists can analyze those data to make predictions about the effects of other changes.

Scientists analyze measurements and observations to answer scientific questions. Analyzing measurements of changes in an ecosystem can provide information about how different parts of the natural system work together.

Measure The temperature of water affects ocean currents and marine habitats. How could scientists get empirical evidence about the temperature of the water? Why is this empirical evidence?

_____

_____

_____

_____

Using Math

Careful measurements are necessary for collecting reliable data. Scientists make measurements several times to be sure that the results can be repeated. In general, scientists use digital instruments to collect quantitative data.

Scientists use mathematics to analyze quantitative data. They record measurements and compare them to find out what changes and what stays the same. A number of measurements can be compared to show if something changes over time. Mathematical analysis can also show how fast a change occurs.

When a scientist makes a claim based on evidence, other scientists can check the claim. When other scientists check the claim and find similar results, the claim or findings are supported by similar evidence.

Evaluate How do numerical data from measurements make it easier to compare results in an investigation?

_____

_____

Research ships carry many instruments that gather data.

Science Practices

Constructing Explanations

After scientists analyze data, they use their results to construct explanations of natural phenomena. A scientific explanation often uses the change in variables to relate one change to another. For example, as conditions in marine ecosystems change, organisms living in the water might change in response. Scientists observe changes in ecosystems and study populations of organisms to learn about effects of changes. Then they construct explanations about the organisms.

Developing and Using Models

Scientists often use models to help them understand something. Models are objects or ideas that represent other things. A model only shows part of the thing that it represents.

Scientists also use computers to make models. You can watch on a computer screen how ocean conditions change over time. The model can show you how plant and animal populations are affected. You can even make a model using words. When you describe something, you are making a verbal model of the object. Other people can learn about the object from your spoken model.

Evaluate How could you make a model to explain how a lobster survives on the ocean floor?

_____

_____

_____

SEP.2 Developing and using models
SEP.6 Constructing explanations and designing solutions
SEP.7 Engaging in argument from evidence

Engaging in Arguments from Evidence

Scientific observations are different from opinions. An opinion is a personal belief and is not always based on facts. An example of an opinion is that tuna tastes better than salmon. No facts support this opinion. An example of a fact is that salmon lay their eggs in fresh water. This statement can be supported by observation.

Scientists use evidence to support their conclusions. For example, the conclusion that whales migrate is based on evidence. Whales can be seen in some areas but not in others, depending on the season. Scientists can also track individual whales to see where they go.

When a scientist makes a claim or argument, other scientists can check the evidence that the claim is based on. Different people making the same observation will find the same evidence. Scientific explanations are always based on empirical evidence.

Explain No one has seen a giant squid with a length of 20 meters. How could scientists use evidence to decide whether these animals exist?

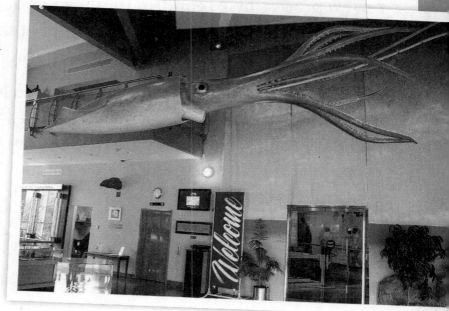

_____

_____

_____

_____

_____

_____

_____

Science Practices

Habits of Mind

Scientists must be creative when they design experiments. Science is focused on answering new questions. That often means that scientists must come up with new ways to answer questions. Designing a good experiment requires them to think of new ways to solve problems. They need to think about what could go wrong and how to fix it. For example, a scientist who studies tiny organisms in the ocean might try to count them using a medical machine that counts blood cells.

When scientists develop new methods, they evaluate them to be certain they are collecting the right data to answer the question. After they have analyzed data and reached a conclusion, scientists share the results. Other scientists then review and evaluate the methods and conclusions. This peer review process helps confirm that investigations were correctly designed. Other scientists may also repeat the investigation to confirm that they obtain the same results.

Plan an Investigation Sea urchins eat a lot of kelp, an underwater organism. A scientist concludes that increasing populations of sea otters would help restore kelp forests because otters eat sea urchins. How could other scientists confirm this conclusion?

_____

_____

_____

_____

Communicate Information

Scientists communicate with other scientists to share what they learned. The words that scientists use sometimes have meanings different from the same word used in everyday communication. *Current, heat,* and *record* are examples of words that have a specific meaning in science. In science, for example, *heat*

Scientists around the world communicate and evaluate results.

refers to the flow of thermal energy. In everyday use, heat may refer to the temperature on a warm day.

Scientists do not perform a single observation or experiment and then come to a conclusion. They repeat experiments and gather the same kind of information. If the results cannot be repeated, then some of the observations may include errors. It is also important that scientific observations can be repeated by other researchers. Sometimes, other researchers cannot get the same result. Then the scientists compare their methods to find out what is different. An error could have happened in one of the methods.

Being able to repeat results makes a conclusion more reliable, so communication among scientists is important. Scientists communicate their methods and results, so other scientists can repeat them and then compare.

Evaluate A scientist repeats an experiment and gets a different result. What should the scientist do next?

_____

_____

_____

Engineering Practices

Defining Problems

Scientists study the natural world. Engineers apply scientific knowledge to solve problems. The first step of the engineering process is stating a well-defined problem. The engineering problem states exactly what the solution to the problem should accomplish. Engineers ask questions to define problems that need to be solved. For example, an engineer might want to build a probe to take samples very deep in the ocean. The engineer might start by asking "What kinds of tools can do that specific job?" Engineers use scientific knowledge and principles to solve the problem.

Before designing a solution, engineers identify criteria and constraints of the problem. The criteria are what the solution must accomplish. For example, one criterion when building a research submarine is that it must work well under the great pressure of the deep ocean. Constraints are limits on the solution. A constraint could be that a solution not go over a certain cost.

Evaluate A classmate says that the cost of an environmental project should not be considered a constraint. Do you agree? Why or why not?

_____

_____

_____

_____

_____

SEP.1 Asking questions (for science) and defining problems (for engineering)
SEP.6 Constructing explanations (for science) and designing solutions (for engineering)
SEP.8 Obtaining, evaluating, and communicating information

Designing Solutions

Before designing a solution, engineers identify criteria and constraints of the problem. For example, one criterion of a solution to rebuild a harbor could be that it restores a habitat for certain animals. A constraint of the harbor restoration could be that it not cost too much money.

Engineers use the criteria and constraints to develop a solution to the problem. They may think of different ways to solve the engineering problem, then decide which way fits the criteria and constraints best.

After they decide on a solution, engineers build the solution and test it. They may use several different design ideas and evaluate each one. They often can combine the best features of each to come to a final design solution.

Design Solutions When ships release water from distant places, they can introduce invasive species. What kind of engineering solution would help prevent the spread of invasive species?

_____

_____

_____

_____

_____

_____

Engineering Practices

Using Models and Prototypes

Similar to scientists, engineers frequently use models as they design solutions. Engineering models can be actual working devices of a proposed solution. Sometimes these devices represent the final solution, but perhaps on a smaller scale. They may only model one part of the solution. Other models are an actual device at full scale and perform all parts of the solution. This kind of model is called a prototype. Engineers use a prototype to collect data that can help them evaluate the design.

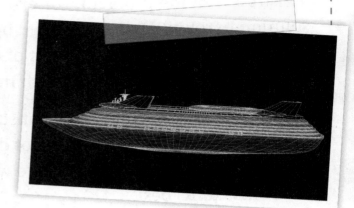

Engineers may use other kinds of models, such as drawings or computer models. A computer model can compare parts of a very complex solution. It allows engineers to make changes and observe what happens without investing a large amount of time or resources to actually build the solution. For example, an engineer investigating ways to restore a damaged ecosystem could use a computer to model changes to the system. The computer could model the effects of changes before the engineer decides which changes to make in a large area.

Infer Why would a computer model of a new ship design save time or money during the construction of the ship?

_____

_____

_____

SEP.2 Developing and using models
SEP.3 Planning and carrying out investigations
SEP.5 Using mathematics and computational thinking
SEP.7 Engaging in argument from evidence

Optimizing Solutions

Engineering is focused on solving problems. A successful solution must meet all of the criteria and constraints. Even if a solution is successful, a better solution may still be possible. When the design is tested, engineers may think of new ideas that might work. The criteria or constraints may also change during the process.

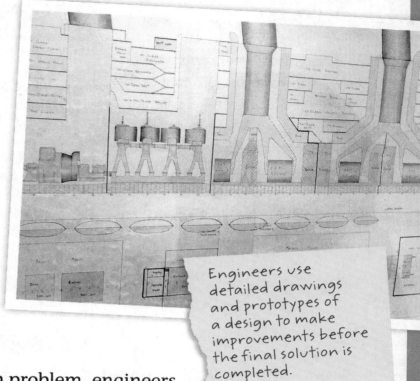

Engineers use detailed drawings and prototypes of a design to make improvements before the final solution is completed.

Even after solving the design problem, engineers continue to work on the solution to optimize it, or make it better. They evaluate the results and consider ways to improve on them. Then they may make a new prototype to determine whether it is a better solution. Like scientists, engineers make a change and then observe or measure the results of the change. After analyzing and evaluating their data, engineers may change the solution or develop a new engineering problem.

Optimize Solutions An engineer designs a project to restore a forest after a mining project. After the design is complete, more funding becomes available. How could the engineer optimize the design solution?

_____

_____

_____

_____

Glossary

The glossary uses letters and symbols to show how words are pronounced. The mark " is placed after a syllable with a primary or heavy accent. The mark ' is placed after a syllable with a secondary or light accent.

adaptation (ad′ āp tā″ shən) a trait that helps a living thing survive in its environment

advantage (ad van″ tij) something that helps

affect (ə fekt″) to change

argue (är″ gyü) to make claims supported by evidence

arid (ar″ id) very dry

atmosphere (at″ mə sfir) the blanket of air that surround a planet

attract (ə trakt″) to pull toward

balanced forces (bal″ ənst fôrs″ əs) two equal forces acting on an object

barometric pressure (bar′ ə met″ rik presh″ ər) the weight of air pushing downward

classify (klas′ ə fī) to sort into groups based on shared traits

climate (klī″ mit) the average weather patterns of a place over a long period

climate change (klī″ mit chānj) change in weather patterns over a long period

condense (kən dens″) to change from a gas to a liquid

conductor (kən duk" tər) a material that electric charges can easily flow through

contact forces (kon" takt fôrs" əs) a push or pull that happens when two objects touch

data (dā" tə *or* dat" ə) facts that can be used to draw conclusions

direction (də rek" shən or dī rek" shən) the way an object faces

distance (dis" təns) how far something travels

diverse (də vėrs") something that comes in many different kinds

dormant (dôr" mənt) a state where a living thing slows its natural activity to survive winter

drought (drout) a long, dry period with little or no rain

electric charge (i lek" trik chārj) a negative or positive charge

electric force (i lek" trik fôrs) the push or pull of charged objects on each other

electromagnet (i lek′ trō mag" nit) a magnet that can be turned on and off with an electric current

elevation (el′ ə vā" shən) the measurement of how high above ground something is

equation (i kwā" zhən) a math problem that shows two equal amounts

equator (I kwā" tər) the imaginary line that divides Earth into a northern half and a southern half

evaporate (i vap" ə rāt) to change from a liquid to a gas

evidence (ev" ə dəns) information that can be used to confirm an idea

exert (eg zėrt") to apply strength or effort

extinct (ek stingkt") the death of all organisms of a particular kind

flood (flud) an overflow of water that spreads over dry land and causes damage

force (fôrs) a push or pull that can act on or change an object

fossil (fos" əl) remains or evidence of plants and animals that lived long ago preserved in minerals

fossil record (fos" əl rek" ərd) total number of fossils found

friction (frik" shən) a force that goes against movement of an object

gravity (grav" ə tē) the force that pulls objects toward each other

Glossary

greenhouse effect (grēn" hous′ ə fekt") the trapping of heat in Earth's atmosphere

greenhouse gas (grēn" hous′ gas) a gas that traps heat in the atmosphere

hibernate (hī" bər nāt) to go into a deep sleep during the winter months

humidity (hyü mid" ə tē) the amount of water vapor in the air

hurricane (hėr" ə kān) a large storm that forms over an ocean with strong winds and a lot of rain

impact (im" pakt) a strong effect

influence (in" flü əns) to have an effect on

inherit (in her" it) to receive a trait from a parent

insulator (in" sə lā′ tər) a material that slows the flow of electric charges

interact (in tər akt") to act or react to something

latitude (lat" ə tüd) a measure of how far south or north of the equator a place is

magnetic field (mag net" ik fēld) the area where a magnetic force acts

magnetic pole (mag net" ik pōl) the point on a magnet where magnetic force is strongest

migrate (mī" grāt) to move from one place to another because the seasons changed

motion (mō" shən) a change in an object's location

natural magnet (nach" ər əl mag" nit) an object that is magnetic without human influence

net force (net fôrs) the total forces acting on an object

neutral (nü" trəl) a material with no electric charge

noncontact force (non" kon′ takt fôrs") a force that acts on an object without touching it

organism (ôr" gə niz′ əm) a living thing

permanent magnet (pėr" mə nənt mag" nit) something that is always magnetic

polar (pō" lər) very cold and dry

position (pə zish" ən) the exact place an object is

precipitation (pri sip′ ə tā" shən) water in the atmosphere that falls to Earth's surface as rain, sleet, snow, or hail

predict (pri dikt") to tell what is likely to happen in the future

relative (rel" ə tiv) compared with

repel (ri pel") to push away

reproduce (rē′ prə düs") to make more organisms of the same kind

source (sôrs) the cause of something

speed (spēd) a measure of how fast or slow something moves

spring force (spring fôrs) force exerted by an object that has been stretched or squeezed

static discharge (stat" ik dis chärj" or stat" ik dis" chärj) the movement of particles with electric charge between objects that are not touching

storm (strôm) a disturbance in the atmosphere that causes large amounts of wind

survive (sər vīv") to continue to live

temperate (tem" pər it) a mild climate with seasonal weather

temperature (tem" pər ə chər) the measure of how hot or cold something is

tension force (ten" shən fôrs) the pulling force that stretches objects

tornado (tôr nā" dō) a large, funnel-shaped mass of swirling wind formed over land

trait (trāt) a characteristic of an organism

tropical (trop" ə kəl) a climate that is warm all year

variation (vâr′ ē ā" shən) a difference in organisms with the same parent

weather (weTH" ər) the conditions in the atmosphere at a particular place and time

Index

* Page numbers for charts, graphs, maps, and pictures are printed in italics.

Illustrations

Articulate Graphics/IllustrationOnline.com; Aaron Ashley Illustration; Kenneth Batelman Illustration; Peter Bull Art Studio; Sara Lynn Cramb/Astound US; Dan Crisp/The Bright Agency; Patrick Gnan/IllustrationOnline.com; Stuart Holmes/Illustration Inc.; Bob Kayganich/IllustrationOnline.com; Matt LeBarre/Blasco Creative, LLC; Melissa Manwill/Shannon Associates, LLC; Mapping Specialists, Ltd.; Bojan Orešković; Precision Graphics/Lachina Publishing Services; Pronk Media Inc.; Rob Schuster; Geoffrey P. Smith; Jim Steck/Steck Figures; Symmetry Creative Productions; Sam Valentino/Bumblecat Design & Illustration, LLC; Ralph Voltz/IllustrationOnline.com

Photographs

Photo locators denoted as follows: Top (T), Center (C), Bottom (B), Left (L), Right (R), Background (Bkgd)

Covers

Front Cover: Spaces Images/Blend Images/Getty Images; Back Cover: Marinello/DigitalVision Vectors/Getty Images;

Front Matter

iii: Pearson Education; iv: Clari Massimiliano/Shutterstock; vi: Wavebreakmedia/Shutterstock; vii: Image Source/Getty Images; viii: Sasils/Shutterstock; ix: Wavebreakmedia/Shutterstock; x: FS Stock/Shutterstock; xi: OLJ Studio/Shutterstock; xii: Microgen/Shutterstock; xiv B: Lakov Kalinin/Fotolia; xiv TR: Barry Tuck/Shutterstock; xv B: Pearson Education; xv T: Pearson Education

Topic 1

000: Danshutter/Shutterstock; 002: Wavebreakmedia/Shutterstock; 005 C: Supannee Hickman/Shutterstock; 005 R: Jennifer B. Waters/AGE fotostock; 006: Bernd Mellmann/Alamy Stock Photo; 009 BC: Wavebreakmedia/Shutterstock; 009 CR: Aptyp_koK/Shutterstock; 012: Goodluz/Shutterstock; 013: Wavebreakmedia/Shutterstock; 014 BR: John Zada/Alamy Stock Photo; 014 CR: Spacephotos/AGE fotostock; 014 L: Corbis/AGE fotostock; 015: Dragon Images/Shutterstock; 016 B: Fotosr52/Shutterstock; 016 BR: BlueSkyImage/Shutterstock; 019 C: Wavebreakmedia/Shutterstock; 019 R: Joseph Scott Photography/Shutterstock; 022: Blickwinkel/Alamy Stock Photo; 023 TL: Wavebreakmedia/Shutterstock; 023 TR: Mediagram/123RF; 024: For Alan/Alamy Stock Photo; 026: Blue Orange Studio/Shutterstock; 027 BR: Inc./Shutterstock; 027 CR: EdBockStock/Shutterstock; 030 Bkgrd: Fotokostic/Shutterstock; 030 BR: Wavebreakmedia/Shutterstock; 031: Tudor Photography/Pearson Education Ltd; 032: Wavebreakmedia/Shutterstock; 034: Everett Collection Inc/Alamy Stock Photo; 035: Hchjjl/Shutterstock; 038 BR: Wavebreakmedia/Shutterstock; 038 TL: Ladyenvy09/Getty Images; 039: Gary Kevin/Dorling Kindersley, Ltd.; 040: Wavebreakmedia/Shutterstock; 041: Destinacigdem/123RF; 042 Bkgrd: BlendMemento/Alamy Stock Photo; 042 CR: Wavebreakmedia/Shutterstock; 043 B: Monkey Business Images/Shutterstock; 043 TR: B. Calkins/Shutterstock; 044 BCR: Simon_g/Shutterstock; 044 BR: Tudor Photography/Pearson Education Ltd; 044 TCR: Tim Hall/Image Source Salsa/Alamy Stock Photo; 044 TR: Vadym Andrushchenko/Shutterstock; 046: Simonovstas/Shutterstock

Topic 2

050: Alex Bartel/Science Photo Library/Getty Images; 052: Image Source/Getty Images; 055 R: Sergei Drozd/Shutterstock; 055 TR: GIPhotoStock/Science Source; 056: Johnnya123/Getty Images; 062 BR: Image Source/Getty Images; 062 L: KingWu/Getty Images; 064: Image Source/Getty Images; 065: Zdenek Kubik/Shutterstock; 066: Stephen Parker/Alamy Stock Photo; 070: Image Source/Getty Images; 072: Image Source/Getty Images; 074 BR: BanksPhotos/Getty Images; 074 CR: Stockbyte/Getty Images; 074 L: Jeremy Walker/SPL/Science Source; 076 Bkgrd: Tinnko/Getty Images; 076 TCR: Image Source/Getty Images; 077 B: Marcin Balcerzak/Shutterstock; 077 TR: Kupicoo/Getty Images; 080: Denim Background/Shutterstock; 083: Hurst Photo/Shutterstock

Topic 3

084: Derek Von Briesen/National Geographic Creative/Alamy Stock Photo; 086: Sasils/Shutterstock; 089: Britt Griswold/NASA; 090: NASA/JPL/University of Arizona/University of Idaho; 092 L: Coffeehuman/Shutterstock; 092 TL: NASA Goddard Space Flight Center Image by Reto Stöckli; 096 Bkgrd: Sunabesyou/Shutterstock; 096 TR: Sasils/Shutterstock; 097 BC: Pongsatorn Singnoy/Shutterstock; 097 BL: Westend61 Hanno Keppel/Getty Images; 097 CR: Roboriginal/123RF; 097 TCR: Shujaa_777/Shutterstock; 097 TL: Sasils/Shutterstock; 097 TR: Mak/Getty Images; 098 BL: Toltek/Getty Images; 098 BR: Welcomia/123RF; 098 C: NZP Chasers/Getty Images; 099: ArtMari/Shutterstock; 100: Blickwinkel/Alamy Stock Photo; 101: Kong Vector/Shutterstock; 102 BL: Della Huff/Alamy Stock Photo; 102 BR: Sasils/Shutterstock; 102 CL: Della Huff/Alamy Stock Photo; 103: Coffeehuman/Shutterstock; 106 B: Phil Ashley/Getty Images; 106 BC: Artur Synenko/Shutterstock; 106 BR: Nnudoo/123RF; 106 L: Sergio Stakhnyk/Shutterstock; 107 CL: NASA; 107 CR: ESA/AOES Medialab; 108 B: Esa Hiltula/Alamy Stock Photo; 108 TL: Sasils/Shutterstock; 109: Jose A. Bernat Bacete/Getty Images; 110: Dpa picture alliance archive/Alamy Stock Photo; 112 BL: Enigma/Alamy Stock Photo; 112 BR: Sasils/Shutterstock; 112 T: Thanapol Kuptanisakorn/Alamy Stock Photo; 114 BC: MarcelClemens/Shutterstock; 114 L: A. T. Willett/Alamy Stock Photo; 115: Picture History/Newscom; 116: Sasils/Shutterstock; 117: Fafarumba/Shutterstock; 118 Bkgrd: Aleksei Kazachok/Shutterstock; 118 CR: Sasils/Shutterstock; 119 B: Batchelder/Alamy Stock Photo; 119 CR: Fedori Nataliia/123RF; 119 TR: Geber86/Getty Images; 125: Makeitdouble/Shutterstock

Topic 4

126: SeppFriedhuber/Getty Images; 128: Wavebreakmedia/Shutterstock; 131 CR: Witold Kaszkin/123RF; 131 R: Anna Jedynak/Shutterstock; 132: Susanne Sims/Photo Resource Hawaii/Alamy Stock Photo; 134 BL: Quick Shot/Shutterstock; 134 CL: Colombo Roberto/Shutterstock; 134 TL: Volodymyr Goinyk/Shutterstock; 135: Vadim Sadovski/Shutterstock; 137 B: Dmitry Kushch/123RF; 137 BC: Wavebreakmedia/

Shutterstock; 138: Pritha Acharya/Alamy Stock Photo; 139: Iakov Kalinin/Shutterstock; 140 TL: Wavebreakmedia/Shutterstock; 140 TR: Mike Theiss/National Geographic Creative/Alamy Stock Photo; 142: Sundry Photography/Shutterstock; 143: Jim Barber/Shutterstock; 146 Bkgrd: LukaKikina/Shutterstock; 146 BR: Wavebreakmedia/Shutterstock; 147: Kletr/Shutterstock; 148: Wavebreakmedia/Shutterstock; 149: National Park Service; 150 BR: Woraatep Suppavas/Shutterstock; 150 C: Boscorelli/Shutterstock; 152 BL: 4045/Shutterstock; 152 BR: Sean Pavone/Shutterstock; 154: Jon Manjeot/Shutterstock; 155: Jatuphon. PTH/Shutterstock; 157 B: Chris Cheadle/Alamy Stock Photo; 157 BC: Wavebreakmedia/Shutterstock; 158: Lockenes/Shutterstock; 159 TR: StevenRussellSmithPhotos/Shutterstock; 160 Bkgrd: Lapandr/Shutterstock; 160 TR: Wavebreakmedia/Shutterstock; 161 B: Dallas and John Heaton/Travel Pictures/Alamy Stock Photo; 161 TR: Mike Theiss/National Geographic Creative/Alamy Stock Photo; 162: Chris Cheadle/Alamy Stock Photo

Topic 5

168: SusaZoom/Shutterstock; 170: FS Stock/Shutterstock; 173 CR: Grigorev Mikhail/Shutterstock; 173 R: Radek Borovka/Shutterstock; 173 TR: Arco Images GmbH/Alamy Stock Photo; 174 BL: Fotofeeling/Zoonar GmbH/Alamy Stock Photo; 174 BR: Bernard Barcos/Alamy Stock Photo; 176 BR: Sarah Jessup/Shutterstock; 176 L: SDM IMAGES/Alamy Stock Photo; 177: Malgorzata Slusarczyk/123RF; 178 BL: SergeUWPhoto/Shutterstock; 178 BR: Theodore Scott/Shutterstock; 179 BC: FS Stock/Shutterstock; 179 TR: Henry Beeker/easyFotostock/AGE fotostock; 182 CL: Stana/Shutterstock; 182 TL: Brad Perks Lightscapes/Alamy Stock Photo; 183 BR: Valentyn Volkov/Alamy Stock Photo; 183 TC: FS Stock/Shutterstock; 184: Fusebulb/Shutterstock; 186: Puhach Andrei/Shutterstock; 187: Zoonar GmbH/Alamy Stock Photo; 188 Bkgrd: Paula French/Shutterstock; 188 BL: Oleksandrum/Shutterstock; 188 BR: Bob Gibbons/Alamy Stock Photo; 189 C: FS Stock/Shutterstock; 189 TR: Tony Mills/Alamy Stock Photo; 190 BL: Eric Isselee/Shutterstock; 190 BR: Aaabbbccc/Shutterstock; 190 CL: Apple2499/Shutterstock; 190 CR: Juha Eronen/Alamy Stock Photo; 190 TCL: Andy Lidstone/Shutterstock; 190 TCR: Dr. Morley Read/Shutterstock; 190 TR: FS Stock/Shutterstock; 191: John Carnemolla/Shutterstock; 192 BC: Chris Sattlberger/Cultura Creative (RF)/Alamy Stock Photo; 192 CL: Sigrid Gombert/Cultura Creative (RF)/Alamy Stock Photo; 192 CR: Fotohunter/Shutterstock; 194: Andrew Lloyd/Alamy Stock Photo; 196 BC: Tom Roche/Shutterstock; 196 L: Tntphototravis/Shutterstock; 197 BC: FS Stock/Shutterstock; 197 R: Beth Dixson/Alamy Stock Photo; 200: Nigel Cattlin/Alamy Stock Photo; 201 B: Caroline Cortizo/Alamy Stock Photo; 201 TL: FS Stock/Shutterstock; 202 Bkgrd: Kevin Wells/Alamy Stock Photo; 202 TR: FS Stock/Shutterstock; 203 B: Monty Rakusen/Cultura Creative (RF)/Alamy Stock Photo; 203 TR: Hero Images Inc./Alamy Stock Photo; 205: Petographer/Alamy Stock Photo; 206 BCL: Herbert Spichtinger/Image Source/Alamy Stock Photo; 206 BCR: Halfmax.ru/Shutterstock; 206 BL: MaraZe/Shutterstock; 206 TL: Joseph/Shutterstock; 206 TR: Maslouskaya Alena/Shutterstock; 209: Lorne Chapman/Alamy Stock Photo

Topic 6

210: Seaphotoart/Fotolia; 212: OLJ Studio/Shutterstock; 215 Bkgrd: Songsak Paname/123RF; 215 BR: Loren Palmer/123RF; 215 CR: Brian E. Kushner/Fotolia; 215 TR: Ktsdesign/Shutterstock; 216: Ghiglione Claudio/Shutterstock; 217: Pung/Shutterstock; 220 BR: OLJ Studio/Shutterstock; 220 CL: Chris Mattison/Alamy Stock Photo; 220 TC: Brandon Alms/Shutterstock; 220 TL: Shchipkova Elena/Shutterstock; 220 TR: Gillian Holliday/Shutterstock; 221 TCR: Geoff Trinder/Ardea/AGE Fotostock; 221 TR: FLPA/Alamy Stock Photo; 222: OLJ Studio/Shutterstock; 223: Lyudmyla Kharlamova/Shutterstock; 224: Dmitrimaruta/Fotolia; 225: Ana Gram/Shutterstock; 229: Alta Oosthuizen/Shutterstock; 230 B: All Canada Photos/Alamy Stock Photo; 231: Otto Hahn/Picture Press/Getty Images; 232: Andrew Pearson/Alamy Stock Photo; 234: Edward Bennett/Design Pics Inc/Alamy Stock Photo; 235 CR: Doug Lindstrand/Newscom; 235 TCR: James Mundy/Alamy Stock Photo; 235 TR: Kwasny221/Fotolia; 238 CR: OLJ Studio/Shutterstock; 238 TL: Pat Canova/Alamy Stock Photo; 239: Martin HughesJones/Alamy Stock Photo; 241: OLJ Studio/Shutterstock; 242 Bkgrd: Yamagiwa/Fotolia; 242 BR: Jim Cumming/Shutterstock; 242 CL: Jag_cz/Shutterstock; 244 Bkgrd: Popoudina Svetlana/Shutterstock; 244 CR: OLJ Studio/Shutterstock; 245 Bkgrd: Elena Elisseeva/Shutterstock; 245 TR: Olaf Doering/Alamy Stock Photo; 246 TL: Davemhuntphotography/Shutterstock; 246 TR: Ana Gram/Shutterstock; 248: Prisma Bildagentur AG/Alamy Stock Photo; 251: Amili/Shutterstock

Topic 7

252: Juergen Ritterbach/Alamy Stock Photo; 254: Microgen/Shutterstock; 257 C: Angie Sharp/Alamy Stock Photo; 257 R: WEJ Scenics/Alamy Stock Photo; 258: Sutichak/Shutterstock; 260: Raylipscombe/Getty Images; 261 BC: Microgen/Shutterstock; 261 CR: Bbtomas/Getty Images; 264 CL: Corey Ford/Stocktrek Images/Alamy Stock Photo; 264 TL: PjrStudio/Alamy Stock Photo; 265: Larissa Pereira/Shutterstock; 266 BR: Mary Evans/Natural History Museum/AGE Fotostock; 266 CR: Sabena Jane Blackbird/Alamy Stock Photo; 266 TCR: The Natural History Museum/Alamy Stock Photo; 266 TL: Microgen/Shutterstock; 267 BCL: Lunewind/Shutterstock; 267 CL: Dinoton/Shutterstock; 267 R: The Natural History Museum/Alamy Stock Photo; 268: William Belknap/Science Source; 270 BR: Microgen/Shutterstock; 270 L: WaterFrame/Alamy Stock Photo; 274: AlessandroZocc/Shutterstock; 275 BCL: Mary Evans/Natural History Museum/AGE Fotostock; 275 BR: Pavel_Klimenko/Shutterstock; 275 CL: Sabena Jane Blackbird/Alamy Stock Photo; 275 CR: Naruedom Yaempongsa/Shutterstock; 275 TCL: The Natural History Museum/Alamy Stock Photo; 275 TCR: Klaus Vartzbed/Shutterstock; 275 TL: Microgen/Shutterstock; 276 BL: Dariush M/Shutterstock; 276 BR: Steve Young/Alamy Stock Photo; 276 CR: Scott Camazine/Alamy Stock Photo; 277: Alicephoto/Shutterstock; 278: Henrik Trygg/Getty Images; 282 BR: Microgen/Shutterstock; 282 TL: Martin Shields/Alamy Stock Photo; 283: Dinoton/Shutterstock; 284: Microgen/Shutterstock; 285 TC: Sabena Jane Blackbird/Alamy Stock Photo; 285 TL: The Natural History Museum/Alamy Stock Photo; 285 TR: Mary Evans/Natural History Museum/AGE Fotostock; 286 Bkgrd: Jane Rix/123RF; 286 CR: Microgen/Shutterstock; 287 B: Reynold Sumayku/Alamy

Stock Photo; 287 TR: Paleontologist natural/Shutterstock; 289: Phaitoon/123RF; 292: The Natural History Museum/Alamy Stock Photo

End Matter

My Notes and Designs

Draw, Write, Create

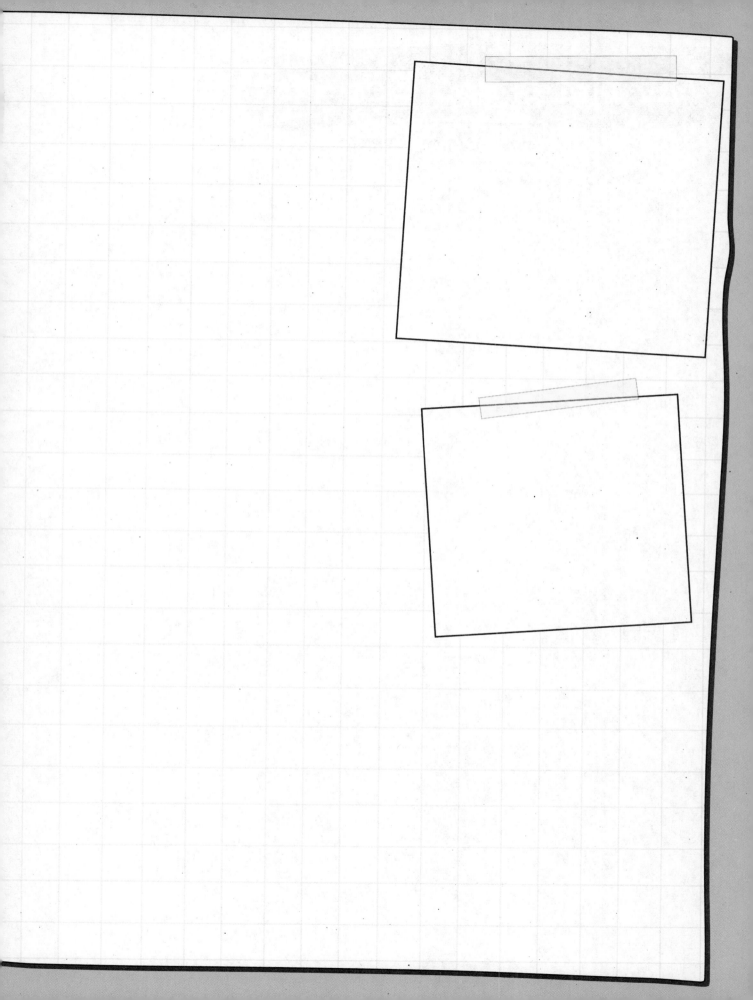

My Notes and Designs

Draw, Write, Create

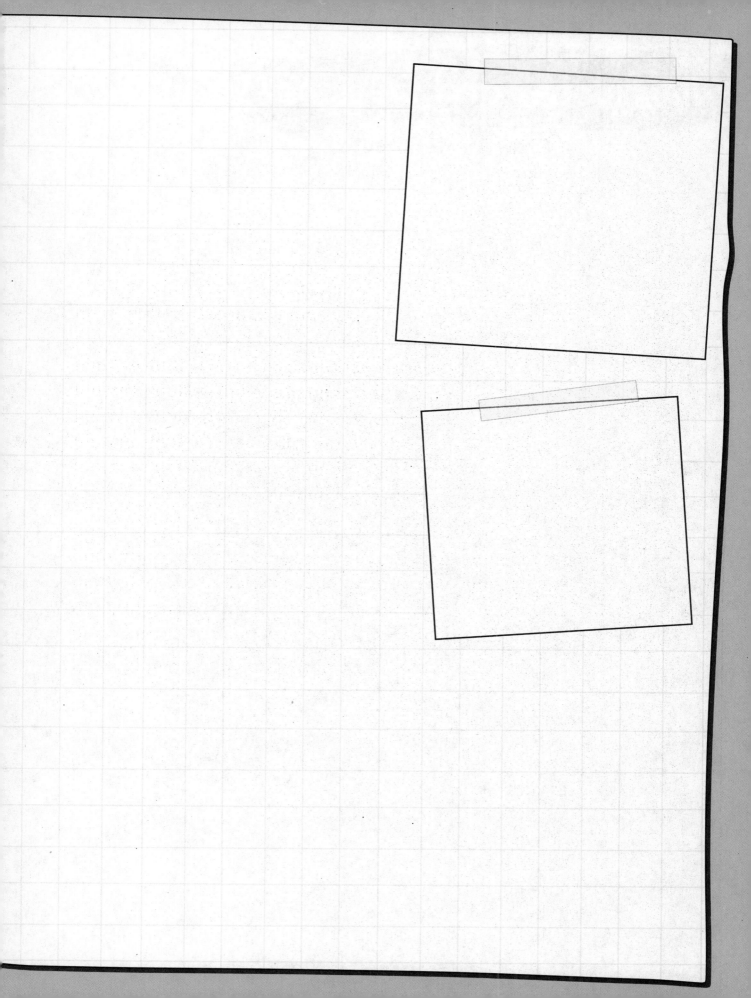

My Notes and Designs

Draw, Write, Create

My Notes and Designs

Draw, Write, Create

My Notes and Designs

Draw, Write, Create

My Notes and Designs

Draw, Write, Create